FROM MISEDUCATION TO INCARCERATION

Dr. Donald R. Evans, Sr.

Milligan Books California

Copyright © 2004 by Dr. Donald R. Evans, Sr.
Los Angeles, California
All rights reserved
Printed and bound in the United States of America

Distributed by:
Milligan Books
1425 W. Manchester Blvd., Suite C
Los Angeles, California 90047
(323) 750-3592
(323) 750-2886 Fax

First Printing, March 2004
10 9 8 7 6 5 4 3 2 1

ISBN # 0-9753504-2-0

No part of this book may be reproduced in whole or in part, in any form or by any means, electronic or mechanical, including photocopying, recording or by any information storage and retrieval system, without permission in writing from the author. Direct all inquiries to Milligan Books

Book Formatting by Chris Ebuehi/Graphic Options Los Angeles, CA

DEDICATION

Dedicated to all those that find themselves in the dark, living in a world that holds you captive against your will, in cultural ignorance, in a racist pit lower than the seventh tier of Dunta's Inferno.

And to those few true New African spirit mates that call out to our Creator, for the strength to bring enlightenment to our criminalized people by upholding the memory of **George Jackson, Shaka Sankofa and Fredrich (Halifu) Pettaway,** who were true New African warriors to the end!!!

Table of Contents

Preface 5
Introduction..7
Chapter 1
    Getting Started 13
Chapter 2
    Moving...33
Chapter 3
    The Joy Of Knowing Thyself 43
Chapter 4
    Finding Afrocentric Education 53
Chapter 5
    Danielle And The DEA...61
Chapter 6
    Disavowing The Addiction To Violence Among
    African-Americans...79
Chapter 7
    How Education, The Afrocentric Way, Works.........85
Chapter 8
    The Loss Of A Daughter..93
Chapter 9
    Shaka's Last Vote..99
Chapter 10
    University Of The Mind 105
Chapter 11
    Functional Illiteracy Is A Killer.............................113
Chapter 12
    The Mirrors In My Soul...119
Chapter 13
    Meeting The Challenge..129

PREFACE

"From Miseducation to Incarceration," compiles the experiences of the senior staff in America's first, and just possibly, its only national Afrocentric prison ministry. It is the result of the vision to support the idea that religion is not the only highway, leading into the inner reaches of a New African's soul.

This selection of essays, lectures, and travel experiences encompass a period of twelve years. This is not an attempt to make a literary statement, where one is not required.

What we see here is the opening of avenues, providing paths for New African inmates to travel, from miseducation through incarceration, back into human revitalization. I have come face to face with functional and cultural illiteracy in its purest form, down right nasty and dirty behind the walls of America's new slave system, the Prison Industrial Complex.

Dr. Donald R. Evans, Sr., is the Chief Executive Officer of the National Association of Brothers and Sisters In & Out (NABSIO), publisher of the Cutting Edge News, and Vice-Chancellor of the George Jackson University.

INTRODUCTION

So many things came into my mind that October 16, 1995, as I stood in the midst of some one million-plus black men, standing in front of the U.S. Capital Building, Washington D.C., waiting for the main speaker. The majority of those in attendance had come to hear, Minister Louis Farrakhan. He, more than all others, will stand face to face with the evil that seeks to destroy the black man on the planet earth, out of love of self and his people.

My spiritual desire was to hear the Minister give a delivery, charged with energy, that would bring me home full of new ideas on how to improve the prison ministry committed to fighting functional illiteracy and cultural ignorance—two of the more serious problems facing black inmates, throughout America's Prison Industrial Complex. The National Association of Brothers and Sisters In & Out, had been struggling with these problems for several years prior to going off to the Million Man March.

If there is one thing you learn early in prison ministry, it's the apathy many black people have towards black inmates. This is not because black people have an inability to show compassion for the downtrodden, but because the power to influence how black people view the Prison Industrial Complex is in the hands of racist and white-supremacy newsmongers. To disregard this influence on how black people feel towards those behind bars, would be and is, a grave mistake.

These were a few of the thoughts that were inside my spirit on that momentous occasion, as the gathering became even more impatient to hear the words of Minister Louis Farrakhan—the one individual in America who could speak to black people in a way no other can. He has the divine words, the power to remove the stigma that is attached to all inmates, especially the black inmate.

So, here I am, standing in the midst of this awesome coming together of black men, the second time I experienced being present and surrounded by a million plus human beings. The other time I was on the Island of Taiwan, during the political days of President Dwight D. Eisenhower, who was paying a visit to one of America's Second World War Allies, General Chiang Kaishek. However, at that million plus gathering, those in attendance were not as joyful as those attending the Million Man March.

I was feeling a debt of spiritual gratitude to Minister Louis Farrakhan, just for living the kind of life he had lived, and joining with the word of God to call forth his brothers to his presence on that blessed day. Nothing that had been available to me throughout my life had ever made the awareness of God as clear to me as did the words of this brother.

I had to question myself, what is it about this man that makes this truth so clear for me? I think it was my ability, thanks to God, to think for myself. I have never needed the press, nor the television, or for that matter some misinformed self appointed community leader, to think for me.

There are many individuals throughout our communities who speak each Sunday. They have a captive audience that sit still in silence, granting these reinforcers of falsehoods the time to spread lies about Minister Farrakhan, unopposed. Because many of them do lie to some of our people, too many I'm afraid, due to your not seeking out the truth for yourself. If a God is telling them that Minister Farrakhan is teaching hatred to our people, it is not "The God" of this universe.

Why must we always be the last ones to see who our true leaders are? Brothers Malcolm, Martin, and Medger did not receive the support from our people they were worthy of, when they were alive. Thus, we contributed to their vulnerability.

On the mall that day, October 16, 1995, I knew this book had to be written. Our people, locked down in prisons across this nation, needed to know that someone had come on their behalf, seeking the spiritual empowerment to forever rid our minds of the fear, and most of all the blinding ignorance, which holds our people to the shackles of white supremacy. Who is it that spreads lies about Minister Louis Farrakhan, so much so, even our own people continue these lies, without even stopping to consider their source?

Our young people deserve to be told the truth. No matter who it hurts. There are far too many African-American youth heading into prison, instead of college. When prison life becomes more glamorous than college life, there is something rotten in Washington, D.C.

I didn't have to travel all across America, to know this nation has never concerned itself about black people, to the degree they truly care how many black youth are behind bars. Hell for that matter, if the truth be told, there doesn't seem to be that many African-Americans themselves that truly care about such matters to the point they are willing to become involved with prison ministries, or are willing to go up against the Prison Industrial Complex, to secure the rights of our people behind bars.

From Miseducation to Incarceration reaches out to all our youth that are desperately seeking truth in the wrong places; reaches out to those beautiful brothers that attended the Million Man March, and those courageous sisters that made it all possible. We realize there is yet much work to be accomplished, and I have faith we will continue to do this work. For the Million Man Marchers that still seek something meaningful to do, prison ministry is a noble cause. We must realize the greatness of any people is found in their love and respect for the <u>truth</u>. The danger of total destruction is hidden in the sugar-coated ignorance concerning our history. It is shameful that we do not utilize our churches that are locked up on Saturdays, to teach the truth about black people to our youth.

    I'd like to digress for a moment, in order to provide some insight into the character of this writer. First, I love this country with a conscious passion that takes in all of the ramifications of the horrific circumstances of the <u>African Holocaust.</u> How could I not love this land that we came to at such tremendous cost, a people that shed many drops of their precious blood in the taming of this America? Their blood will never be dismissed lightly. Not as long as one descendent is alive, that knows the awesome price paid by African people coming through the Middle Passage into this land of constant lies and denial.

    Like our Native American brothers concerning their American Holocaust, and our Jewish brothers concerning their Holocaust, we understand when they tell us <u>NEVER AGAIN!</u> If you would ask any conscious black man about those two Holocausts, he will likely tell you they pale by comparison. This in no way seeks to demean the sacrifices these two great people experienced, at their extremely high human cost. But, the African Holocaust was both horrific in cruelty and astronomical in duration. Not only should we say <u>NEVER AGAIN,</u> we must insist the debt owed the black American be paid. Only then will we finally know the true meaning of the ancient saying, "African, know thyself." You too, will come to understand how I can love this country with a conscious passion.

All people who love and respect their culture, can understand when the African says, "I came before all others, and I am, because I am."

Chapter 1

GETTING STARTED

The legendary blues master B.B. King, of Indianola, Mississippi, laments in his recording, "Why I Sing the Blues," "The first time I got the blues, I was coming over on a ship, and men were standing over me with whips." After hearing this song, there should be no doubt the foundation had already been laid for the coming of the Black Holocaust, during the Middle Passage.

Each time I hear this recording, I think to myself, "Being shackled in a space no larger than my body size, in a stench so vile, fresh air refused to enter this hellhole of human degradation, the

FROM MISEDUCATION TO INCARCERATION

waves from the Atlantic continuously making gallant attempts to wash this genocidal behavior from existence, continues to haunt my thoughts." This makes me question, is there any room for doubt, that the Middle Passage was an early incubator for the blues of the Black Holocaust?

This book wanted to start a hundred other places, places where the ugly face of incarceration has taken me, over the past ten years. In fairness to each of these other high points, in what has come to be the most rewarding ten years of a truly worthwhile life, I am satisfied this began where it did. My life has always provided me with struggles, so I am never far from this traditional music of the black American, 'The Blues.' This book could not come to life without my paying respect to the black man's traditional music. It goes without saying, we do indeed have a spiritual reason to sing the blues.

The inspiration to write this book didn't come from some voice deep inside my brain. Nor was I inspired by our Creator placing it on my heart. I can't even claim my ancestors were standing at my ear, whispering instructions to me. The truth of the matter is I became 'pissed,' once I found out black inmates were crying out, lifting their voices into a tornado of silence, requesting Afrocentric literature and a sense of history to help cope with being locked down, and struggling mightily to maintain their sanity. Locked down, and in many cases treated as inhumanely as the law will allow. There is an empowering transformation, when the black American adult first starts to learn the truth about his people, the truth about his motherland, the truth as it is written by scholars that look like him.

In my case this empowering transformation was so wonderful, I have not stopped growing in spirit from the moment I knew for certain what was happening to me. I have come to know myself for the first time. Perhaps this is part of the reason I felt so 'pissed,' real-

GETTING STARTED

izing there are those who wished to keep black inmates from having access to the source of their own 'truth.'

This information was provided to me by a former inmate, who was recently released from the prison that housed such notorious criminals as Charles Manson and Sirhan Sirhan—Corcoran State Prison. Where these criminals are housed has minimal interest for me. What is of interest to me is Corcoran State Prison itself. To house inmates of their status, you need guards at this facility that are willing to go the limit in their inhumane treatment of inmates.

This is the facility that held a young black inmate that would become my mentor on prison matters. Never having been inside a prison facility, my knowledge up to this point, had been acquired from movies dealing with prison life.

I give credit to Brother Kenneth Madden, who at one point in his young life used to awaken to the harsh reality of prison bars in his face each morning. This brother, having met me only through the words we exchanged in our letters, agreed to become my mentor, to assist me in seeing how the California Department of Corrections (CDC) carries out its job of dealing with a large number of black inmates.

From behind the 'razor wire enclosure' my training started with a growing number of letters in the handwriting of inmates. Letters providing as much information as it was possible to convey, without bringing the system down on their heads for letting too much information escape to the outside. Without prison staff reading each letter that comes from behind the iron bars of Corcoran State Prison, sooner or later truth about the treatment of black inmates, was destined to get out.

It's one thing to be in prison physically, yet another situation to lose your mind to the same madness that is holding your body captive. All that have been touched by me have our Spiritual Father to thank, for granting Brother Madden the ability to see this vision of hope in the midst of his prison madness, as we shared through letter writing. It was his faith and beliefs that gave birth to the idea that it was possible to do something to help inmates gain a true picture of self.

My letters continued to pile up. Some were of such deep thoughtfulness that I started sharing them with my co-workers at the postal facility where I worked. They were all impressed, but, not to the degree that they wanted to become involved with writing to inmates. Thus, my dilemma became a question—"Where do I go from here?"

Fortunately this question was not as difficult to deal with, as I was making it out to be in my mind. I was coming closer to having this question answered, although I didn't realize it at the time. At the next meeting of the Community Financial Investment Group (CFIG), I discovered what my next step should be.

CFIG held its weekly meetings on Florence Avenue, several blocks west of Van Ness Boulevard. At their next meeting, I took a stack of the best letters, as far as clarity and stated purpose, to expose them to the group.

The members were very cooperative and agreed to read all of the letters before giving me a hearing in order to offer their advice. This was more than I had hoped to gain at this meeting. Finally, I was given the opportunity to express how I came to be in possession of these letters. In as few words as possible, I gave them the facts surrounding my writing the first letter to inmate Kenneth Madden, how he was willing to become my teacher, providing the facts needed for me to gain a little knowledge of how it felt to be locked down, and not having Afrocentric books to help retain your sanity while incarcerated. My guess is that I made my case, because their advice to me was I should go forward and start providing positive Afrocentric literature for our people in prison.

GETTING STARTED

At this meeting, not only did I receive sound advice that changed my life, I found, or I should say he found me, the last element of this vision, Nathaniel Perkins-Ali. Not only did his level of understanding of what I was heading into become immediately apparent, he willingly stepped forward to give of himself to assure the success of our program. Now the baby vision had moved into the last stage of the birth cycle.

What Ali brought to the table was stamina, style, literary ability—and most important of all, he came with a faith so strong, it caused my mind to recall the Biblical words of Jesus Christ, when he was talking about Peter the Apostle, "On this rock I will build my church."

The next several days we spent getting to know one another, and talking with other grassroots organizations that already had their non-profit status. We started working out the details of just what we hoped to accomplish.

In my next letters to my inmate teachers, I introduced Brother Ali, and told them of his willingness to assist in organizing our vision into a reality. Soon there were as many letters coming to Brother Ali, as there was coming to my mailbox—which gave us little, or no time, to work on organizing. Thus, it became necessary to cut down on our letter writing, in order that we could spend more time in chartering the organization.

First, we developed a statement of purpose, outlining what we planned to accomplish with this organization. It soon became clear, we had a very stressful situation on our hands. Days became weeks and weeks became months, and still no news from the Secretary of State, on the status of our organizational papers. They had to be approved at the state level before we could ask the federal government for their approval.

FROM MISEDUCATION TO INCARCERATION

Nevertheless, we did not stand idly by, twiddling our thumbs, while we waited for the stroke of the pen, that would make our organization a legal tax-free entity in the world of Afrocentric activism.

We had no budget to work with, just a vision of what should and could be, when blacks stand up for what we know to be right and just. We were determined to not let others always have the last word, as to how our tax monies are spent—such as a mad rush to continue building prisons, in order to warehouse an increasing number of oppressed people, that often get ensnared in traps woven by the rich, and powerful. The power that be were seeking to become even more powerful through the new slave making laws.

Several more weeks of meeting new brothers through the mail passed before word came back from the Secretary of State, requesting additional information be provided, before a decision could be rendered.

After compiling the additional information requested, we went back to the business office where we had contracted their services to get our organization chartered. Not having a budget posed another problem. We could not meet the price they were requesting to continue to keep us as their clients.

The decision was made that we would complete the necessary action ourselves. At the time I was still working full-time for the Los Angeles Bulk Mail Center in Bell, California, which placed most of the workload of getting our papers in order—on the shoulders of Brother Ali—a challenge he willingly met.

My challenge was to work as many overtime hours as possible, in order to finance this vision that was born somewhere inside my spirit. I, too, accepted my part willingly.

Within the week our papers were returned to the Secretary's office. Keeping pace with this action, other areas continued to show progress. Organizational literature was developed around the 'mission statement,' submitted to the state government for approval. The mission statement detailed our purpose, telling anyone that cared to read it, this is where our energy will be spent in the words of our quest, "Let every prison become a university, and every prison-cell become a classroom for Afrocentric study."

My mentor was busy pushing this vision throughout the general population, selecting brothers that wanted to share this vision. There were many brothers that came to know me, and about me. Two stood head and shoulders above the others that were corresponding with me at the time—one because of his burning desire to teach other inmates the unlimited possibilities of understanding self, and acquiring Afrocentric knowledge, knowledge that could help to change the plight of locked-down black men, throughout this nation. He because the director of education, with the power to develop our very first curriculum, which made our vision more a reality than an idea.

Even now as he fights against the board of prison term, to regain his release date, he still finds time to assist any of his fellow inmates, who reach out requesting his help in the area of education.

The second brother, you could truthfully say, was one the system wanted to be rid of. He was a thorn in their side, one that would never ask for, nor grant any quarter. If the system was found to be violating any California Department of Correction policies, he would be among the first to expose the violations. It didn't matter the system would come down on him with some form of punishment, they could not break his will to fight back.

Many of the prisons in the state are located right in the middle of some large farming situation, where it is necessary to use 'crop dusting' aircraft, for the purpose of spraying some form of pesticide on the crops, eliminating unwanted pests. On more than one occasion, the pilots would fail to turn off the chemical dispensing apparatus, as they came to the boundary of the farm, which made the chemicals fall into the prison yard, where any prisoners in the general population, for that period, would be exposed to whatever dangerous chemical was being used at the time.

When no medical treatment was given to inmates that requested to be treated, some of the inmates that could not be threatened into silence concerning such treatment, or the lack thereof, would seek to get the word outside of the prison. This is how I came to have knowledge of this violation of prison rights. Not only was I given this information, many others on the outside had been given the same information. I felt it should receive some space in a newspaper.

The publisher of the Community Circle Newspaper was under the same impression, once she read the article in my possession, sent by one of the brothers at this California Department of Correction facility. It received top billing in this grassroots newspaper.

When I got a copy of the newspaper, I rushed over to the nearest post office to mail a copy to the inmate that provided the article. I was told it caused more than a little confusion in the mailroom, once they knew what they had in their hands.

The inmate was questioned thoroughly concerning the article. Then, not getting the results they had hoped for, the inmate was put in isolation for refusing to cooperate with the prison officials wanting information on this matter. One way to know you had won a battle, was by the system's reaction to the news that they were exposed for having violated their own policies.

Unscrupulous political individuals creates the conditions making it possible for the mistreatment of inmates by writing laws the majority of the voters are willing to vote into law, as long as the oppressed are kept locked down, or kept within the boundaries of America's inner cities. So what if some inmates are sprayed with some dangerous chemicals, who cares?

Many of those that write to our organization are individuals who still have much to offer the community. If only we as a people, a concerned black people, can somehow find within ourselves positive Afrocentric energy, we can encourage our people not to give up the struggle in the midst of the battle.

Not long after this story was published in the Community Circle Clipper Newspaper, the inmate who was provided the information was transferred to another facility where he stayed until his release. However, he continued to help shape our organizational philosophy. He also developed the first logo for our organization.

We rented office space on South Western Avenue, Los Angeles, with the Community Financial Investment Group. During that time our ideas, and the inputs, that was coming from behind prison walls throughout the state, increased.

An inexpensive computer was bought from CFIG, because they were upgrading their office equipment. This made it possible for Brother Ali to finalize all of the necessary office and organizational literature required to stabilize our sense of legitimacy, many days prior to the arrival of our approved charter.

There was a strong feeling we were on the right path, heading into a whirlpool of Afrocentric reality, black men standing tall for the truth that nothing is being accomplished to help change the lives of those in criminal lifestyles. Education is the key to this unwillingness to face the reality of greed, and the always present ignorance of self, that is so prevalent among African-American inmates.

This is the area where our organization feels the real fight against crime in the inner city must be fought. The way is clear, the battlefield

FROM MISEDUCATION TO INCARCERATION

is right before us. The enemy is known. Thus, we must rally those brothers, and indeed our 'locked-down' sisters that wish to join this struggle to encourage a sense of Afrocentric pride, within the walls of America's prisons.

Many blacks are prone to stand on the sidelines, unwilling to get involved with forging change in the world they live in, letting others dictate how they live and breathe, even more a prisoner than those behind the walls of America's Prison Industrial Complex that seek to keep Africans born to this land, in what white power brokers see as 'our' place.

A certain number of blacks know there is an army of our people 'locked-down' in America. Not just an army of criminals, but an army of the best minds coming out of the inner cities of this nation. They have rights that are often overlooked, based on what the mass media projects.

Word was spreading throughout the California prison system about the coming of our organization, due in part to families we came in contact with in and about Los Angeles. It is safe to say, "Two out of every five adult African-Americans living in the inner cities, either have a relative behind bars, or they know someone that does." This is the reason those in the activist community often state with a high degree of certainty, that black people are being returned to slavery at an alarming rate, by the use of corrupt and unjust laws and the criminal justice system.

Our next step was to recruit a number of volunteers that would be willing to serve on our board of directors. We first looked to our families for assistance. Next we turned to our friends. Then we looked into the Los Angeles activist community to see if there were those there willing to join our team. There were individuals in each of these arenas that came forward to give of their time.

With a board in place, it became easier to plan for the coming programs. While the board was learning what their duties would involve, other ideas were being introduced to our small staff. Advice is often given, so long as there is no requirement to do the work necessary to implement the idea. However, we never rejected any ideas that were suggested on how best to operate this prison ministry. One thing was certain, we were heading into uncharted waters because there was no other Afrocentric prison ministry on the horizon. We had the field all to ourselves, from what we were being told by those writing from behind prison walls.

This concept for prison ministry was to be different from day one in that it was not a ministry in the sense of teaching religion. In keeping with the definition of the term 'ministry,' to 'serve' was our mission. All throughout our lives we have had religion handed to our people from the plantation to the penitentiary. Still, for many Africans born in America, there is something missing from this equation. Our contention, is that the missing link is freedom from ignorance, ignorance that is as dangerous as racism to the well-being of today's black American.

Putting forth a program that would become attractive to the thinkers among black inmates became our charge. These were the inmates that could understand that not knowing themselves, not having a strong sense of racial identity based on knowledge presented by our own scholars, made it easy to be used by those that peddled racism as a way of life.

Fighting against the Prison Industrial Complex is exhausting work. Much labor is spent trying to stop the building of more prisons, and we still have little to show for it. For the black American, far greater than for any other group, there is an urgent need to understand the power we have as a people to withdraw from the discipline of ignorance.

We to look inward for solutions to many of the problems we face as a people. Crime is as much a weapon being used against black America, as is lack of education, poor health protection, and low self-esteem. All of these are players in the evil game confronting the black American. It is not so much the prison industrial complex that is our enemy, as the slavery we hold within which feeds the inferior way many black Americans see themselves. Gone are the days when fear of bringing dishonor upon one's family, even if it would cause harm to one's self, was enough to stop some individuals from breaking the law. There was a time when being sent to prison was not seen as something to be proud of.

There are yet great thinkers among black people in America. If only these thinkers would put self aside, put religion as it is known in America in the background, and become nation minded, long enough to get the majority of blacks on the same page, perhaps, then and only then, could an Afrocentric agenda evolve that could, in the coming years, hasten the return of our collective sense of greatness. We need to offset the system's constant propaganda demonizing Americans that are powerless to mount any defense to counteract this racist arrogance. All the more reason why we need a collective black agenda. Now!

Without a national push for Afrocentric education by Africans in America, for all school age children, this saga will continue to play out in favor of those in the power position, that see it to their advantage to criminalize a greater percentage of black youth, than is being college trained. This is one of the primary reasons why the incarceration rate among black youth continues to increase. The greater the numbers of black inmates, the fewer the number of jobs needed to keep the lid on America's so-called 'melting pot,' that seems to melt for all but the black man.

For more than a few years I have worked to come to an understanding in my mind, an understanding of why it is that many blacks are willing to wait until they die for their reward to be granted. I am not convinced that it would anger the God of the African, if we should pay a lot of attention to 'here and now,' and 'less attention to the hereafter.' There is enough evidence available to convince any individual, that whatever the black man's working collectively thing is, it isn't working to his advantage.

This is the strongest point to be made for teaching Afrocentric studies—being knowledgeable enough about the behavior of black Americans that one can see from the available evidence that more needs to happen, if the descendants of former slaves are destined to brighter days. Stop to think, what could be if only we stop trying to be something that our Creator didn't see fit to make us—white.

To reverse the behavior of achieving incarceration instead of education, much study is required to find the root cause of this negative phenomenon, aside from the system's racist treatment in demonizing its black citizens. The answer to this question can possibly be found among the large number of black inmates—many of whom highly intelligent, with time on their hands, and truly wish to give back something positive to their communities. To make this reasonably possible, much is required of those that wish to extend a helping hand to those behind bars. Great change can occur when the minds of concerned black Americans are fed up with things as they are, and decide this can no longer be, which is how our organization feels.

Inmate Jackson, at our suggestion, had volunteered to write a curriculum for our Afrocentric correspondence course, complete with the number of textbooks required. Study guides for each text were also written by our first education director, which made it easier to implement our program. All of this material was presented to our

FROM MISEDUCATION TO INCARCERATION

office ready to be printed up, so we could enroll our first inmate students. The next step was to write one hundred question multiple choice tests for each text used in the curriculum. These tests were to be administered as closed book exams, administered after the satisfactory completion of each text with its study guide. Most of this work was mine to accomplish, due to the workload already assigned to Brother Ali.

The task was necessary because we needed a way of knowing how much knowledge our students retained after completing their assigned text and study guide. Since the area of Afrocentric studies is one of my majors, I welcomed this assignment to put this knowledge to good use, to help others to understand the joy of knowing their true history. The great culture of black Americans should be known and appreciated by all, for its shaping of world culture is a blessing in and of itself. All of these major points were written into all materials produced by our staff.

The intent here was to do all in our power to use knowledge to fight low self-esteem. We looked for ways to elicit the help of our inmate students in finding answers to some of the many problems confronting large numbers of African-Americans living behind bars. Oftentimes the opportunity to make a difference is right before our eyes. Many refuse to see these opportunities for fear of getting involved, because getting involved would require revealing our weakness. In today's world there is no room for those that are full of fear of the system. Whatever is a flaw in our make-up must be overcome. It is no mystery that the black American prays for deliverance as much as he does; we cannot long survive as an important people, if we continue to fear getting involved in combating the many killers of the black spirit.

This organization is not just some grassroots group that seeks to protest, just for the sake of argument. It is more, much more. We realize black Americans are in the midst of a war, not of their making. Yet, it is a war that is killing our youth, and miseducating a large majority of the ones that escape death. Too many are incarcerated who are among our strongest assets. Many of those in our midst still pray for some mystical change. Some pray that goodness will enter the hearts of those making war against the people they still view as less than human.

Afrocentricity inspires us to look to ourselves to save our people, to not wish to be what we are not, and never will be, no matter how great the effort. We cannot afford to lose great numbers of our collective family, as if it doesn't matter. It does matter, not only to the immediate family, it must matter to the collective as well. One does not hand over great numbers of soldiers in a war to the enemy, and still hope to continue to fight. If we know nothing else, we know our Creator did not place us on this planet, for the purpose of being slaves to anyone. This truth we must teach our young, so they can reflect this teaching in their behavior and their peer group relationships.

One cannot help but be blinded by the glitter and glamour of ignorance, when there is a critical lack of teaching to the contrary. It is ignorance that keeps the black American thinking he needs a gun in his home for protection, drugs in his possession in order to make a living, and no education in order to gain respect among peers. One cannot find the road to love, without understanding that love is also found in ones' pride in being part of a great people. No one can deny that black American has withstood all that racism has presented down through the years, and is still standing.

This question was reported in an edition of the Shreveport Sun, a city newspaper, "If you know the system is blatantly unjust, why do you put yourself in harm's way?" This question was asked by State Senator

FROM MISEDUCATION TO INCARCERATION

Don Cravins, D-Arnaudville. I would ask a different question, "When will we take action to eliminate the unjust laws which are used to continue incarcerating blacks that are targeted for arrest?" The system is unwilling to accept any blame for the increased number of inner city youth, trapped in socio-economic pits of racism, that are sent to jail rather than to college.

There are those that feel a university is a group of buildings, off in some beautiful green surroundings, where higher learning takes place. Is it possible to see prisons through the same mind's eye, as a place where higher learning can occur? Our organization looks at prisons with this thought in mind. This is the program we shall continue to market throughout the California prison industrial complex, until a better plan is devised.

The journey from slavery to freedom was fraught with danger; death often awaited any wrong step. Still Conductor Tubman, of Underground Railroad fame, kept pushing forward, no amount of danger could sway her from her objective. Do we desire freedom less today, than in the days of her gallant struggle? Are we telling the world the courage of the black American is so eroded by drugs, incarceration, self-hatred, broken families, miseducation, poor health protection, racism and ignorance, that we fear the collective journey from "ignorance to Afrocentric knowledge?"

The whip is still in the hands of those found standing over the black American, as blues master B.B. King tells us, in "Why I sing the blues." We are yet singing the blues, but our courage is still intact, if we would but use it.

The ships that are carrying our people to their death are no longer made of wood. Many of these ships are so small they are beyond human sight. They are no less dangerous than the ships that crossed the Middle Passage. They do not carry the names of some famous

GETTING STARTED

persons. These ships are called HIV and AIDS, drugs and guns, ignorance and miseducation, black on black crime, self-hatred and low self-esteem, unjust criminal courts and mass incarceration. These are slave ships that never leave port without a full cargo of oppressed people, sailing through a Middle Passage of racism, into an ocean of white supremacy.

There are those in the black community that have the means to help our inmates, but these same individuals lack the will to do so. It is easy to visit a prison, when the business is promoting Christianity. When will it become clear, the black inmate needs something more than the teachings of Christianity? He needs the teachings that will cause him to see himself in another setting, a setting where he has a good paying job, that will let him be the man that he so desperately wishes to be. This is not to put down religion, it's stating that we need to see our problems from a different perspective.

Crime, in any situation, is big business. What the majority of blacks that live the life of crime fail to realize, is the fact that this business needs for him to continue his criminal behavior at the level he does, in order to support their lifestyles. The truth of this revelation is seen in the opposition offered by the prison industrial complex to any positive program for change, if they are not the ones to evolve the plan.

Afrocentricity is a very mistrusted word, not only among whites within the prison system, it can also cause mistrust among those within the black community, among those that still feel comfortable with the term "Negro." Keeping blacks in a consciousness that finds no fault in being typed as a negro, holds the African closer to the condition of slavery. Any black person that does not have a free mind will, no doubt, consider himself a "Negro" in order the please the ones with power over him.

FROM MISEDUCATION TO INCARCERATION

Once the mind is free of caring what the enemy thinks, one is then free to think for himself. In thinking for yourself you have an undying obligation to name yourself.

Dr. Molefi Kete Asante in his text, "Afrocentricity" writes that, "Afrocentricity is the belief in the centrality of Africans in postmodern history. It is our history, our mythology, our creative motif, and our ethos exemplifying our collective will."

No other can sing the black man's blues, like he can. Try though they may, there is always something missing. Don't try to cry my tears when I'm the one with the pain. Dr. King gave a clear example of this point in his "Letter From a Birmingham Jail" when, he defined just laws as those which were in keeping with the laws of God, and unjust laws as those which violated human dignity.

How can the ones that give us unjust laws understand my song? Even the ones that wrote to Dr. King, while he was locked down in a Birmingham jail, who claimed to be men of God, could not truly see where Dr. King was coming from. How could they when their hearts were not at the level where Dr. King's was. It is impossible for them to feel empathy for him.

There is a great need for this organization to lift the self-esteem of the African behind bars. It will remain the responsibility of our genius to find ways to bring our scholars in contact with those who are locked down in America.

In order to bring those inmates home in the frame of mind to be builders for a more secure community, the inmate must come to know and understand the importance of Dr. Karenga's work. Karenga's work," according to Dr. Asante, must be studied for its inherent consistency of thought and purpose.... His strength exists in his cultural work which utilizes the seven criteria: history, mythology, creative motif, ethos, social organization, political organization, and economic organization." (Asante, 1998)

This information must be told, and retold, to our brothers and sisters living their lives behind bars. It is not enough to say we believe in the teachings of Christianity, if we are unwilling to educate our locked down people, that they may decide for themselves the true value of teaching Moses and Karenga.

We are now started, let us move forward on the path of Afrocentricity, where I vow to sing my own blues.

Chapter 2

MOVING FORWARD

One thing becomes clear right away in dealing with our people locked down, there's much more work required just to keep up with the incoming letters. This point was always made clear to any audience I was fortunate enough to address. I didn't start this organization because God had moved me in that direction. If He did, I wasn't aware of it. Receiving the volume of mail that was coming to our mailbox, and understanding how appreciative inmates are to have someone write to them, started working on my state of mind. My spirit was renewed after feeling these words that leaped off the pages of so many letters.

FROM MISEDUCATION TO INCARCERATION

Brother Ali, the other half of our idea for the organization, was the first to think it through that we need help in keeping up with our incoming letters. However, we didn't want our people in prison to think we were interested in operating a matchmaking service. Our objective must remain clear, education is the organizational goal and will remain so. Whenever a letter was received requiring a female pen pal, that person would be reminded of our purpose.

After Brother Kenneth Madden was made aware of our dilemma, he made it possible for a committee made up of two board members, and two staff members, to meet with his mother. The purpose of this meeting was to find out if she would be willing to organize a letter-writing group.

This meeting took place at the Burger King, on Avalon and El Segundo Boulevards, in Compton, California. It was a very good meeting that lasted some two hours. She was very impressed with the idea of helping to make the lives of her son, and others, a little easier by writing to them. Also, she was willing to bring other women into the organization, in order to help register our new inmate students.

After Mrs. Madden joined our staff, I was able to spend more time writing pre-tests, and the end of text exams. Whenever a potential inmate student would contact our office, requesting information on becoming a part of our student body, we would respond by sending an introductory letter. Enclosed with this letter would be an enrollment form, that gave a brief narrative of what our educational goals were, and what we looked for in our students. We made sure we encouraged them to remain disciplinary free, if at all possible, while they were enrolled in our program. Once they had received this introductory information, and decided they wanted to join our student body, by completing the enrollment form and mailing it back to our address, they would receive a 50 question multiple-choice pre-enrollment test accompanied by a letter of congratulation. This pre-enrollment test was not given for the purpose of awarding a grade. We used this as a tool to indicate just how much our new students already knew about the history of our people.

We encouraged all of our students to write as often as they had questions. This went well for the ones that were better educated. For so many people in prison, functional illiteracy is a grave problem. The problem is so severe, many inmates must have other inmates to read, and respond to, the letters they receive from family and friends. We are still looking for a way to tackle this problem in a way that will make a difference.

One way we determined would help to collect the data needed to advance this ministry, was to develop a program of sending staff members into the prisons to teach our program in person, not realizing at the time, this was easier said than done. Still we made our plans as if we already had been given clearance to visit any prison of our choice.

This is not how this program came to develop behind bars. In the prisons where blacks are employed that have a higher sense of Afrocentric pride, you are more than likely to receive better cooperation. This is how it is at the Federal facility, located at the Terminal Island Prison, in San Pedro, California.

One of my activist associates recommended me as a possible speaker for their program, to be held in the month of February, honoring Black History. When I received a call from one of the staff persons, extending an invitation to come speak on this occasion, I readily accepted.

It has been my experience that our people are more receptive to a speaker, if that speaker speaks from his mind and heart, not having to depend on notes or a prepared paper. This is my style when appearing before an audience, where the subject is dealing with the history or the culture of black people.

I arrived some thirty minutes early to get cleared to enter the prison. The staff person coordinating the event was not there to meet me. He had given the front desk instructions that I was to fill out the necessary data sheet, go through the electronic testing device, then have a seat until he came to escort me into the facility. There were others there waiting for the same purpose, to attend this event. We didn't have long to wait before the Muslim Minister was there, introducing himself, and giving a brief overview of what to expect on the inside.

I learned that the correct way to address a Muslim Minister is by the title Imam. There was so much that I needed to know about what was going on in the world behind bars. I realized at that point that my education was just beginning.

Each speaker was allotted fifteen minutes to make our presentation. I was to speak third on the program. The first to speak was the female director of a grassroots organization known for its interest and concern in protecting our children. The name of this organization is Mothers Reclaiming our Children (MROC). She was a very good speaker, and held the interest of her audience with what she had to say, which was plenty. She told how her group made many trips to the criminal courts in Los Angeles, and throughout the metropolitan areas that comprise the Los Angeles County Court System.

This system is reported to be the largest in the world. If this system only prosecuted black and Hispanics, it would still be the largest in the world. Each day there is someone being brought before the court, that will be sent to prison for many years of their lives, not because they are guilty of breaking the law, as much as they are guilty of being poor. Poverty in America is a crime. Poverty is relegated to

MOVING FORWARD

the 'have-nots' in America, the part of America that has little, or no say, in the laws that they often stand accused of breaking. The passing of laws in America is in the hands of those that have the ability to defend themselves, in the very courts they themselves operate.

The audience was being informed about something they had learned firsthand, of just how little justice is found in this system. Often when they are arrested, it is the first time they start getting information that could have made a difference in their choices. They are ensnared by laws passed just for the purpose of controlling the victims of poverty—the poor. This was nothing new to the majority, many had been before the courts several times, and knew the speaker was telling the truth. What was new was the fact that standing before them was someone who cared. Someone who had on many occasions gone before the courts, on behalf of some mother's child, seeking to keep him from wasting away in prison. She told them of the pain she felt, each time she appeared in court, not so much because of the insensitive attitude of the courts, but because of the pain caused by the defendant's lack of knowledge of the system that had judged him. Many were inspired by her words, because I'm certain in their minds, the words were coming forward as if from their own mothers. I know this is how I felt.

The main point she wanted to impress upon them, was they must not feel that there is no one that cared about them, aside from their own families. She spoke about how far we have come as a people, and how far we have yet to travel. We will not get to our journey's end in good shape, if we cannot recapture the collective ability we shared as a people coming forward from slavery, the ability to love ourselves, and each other.

She told how the vultures from among the 'haves' are preying upon the weak among our people. One way to prevent this from continuing at such a high rate, is to join grassroots organizations, and become involved in helping to correct some of these problems. She told them to contact their families, tell them about the things she told them at this meeting and invite them to come to her organization's weekly meetings that are held to inform the public how they too can become involved.

At the conclusion of her speech she received a standing ovation—one that was well deserved, due to the information and sense of caring she conveyed to her audience.

The Imam came forward to request another round of applause for a very moving speech. These inmates knew they had received much love in the words they had heard, and they required very little prompting from the Imam, to give an inspired response.

When the next speaker was introduced, I suddenly realized I had met this brother some months ago at a rally on behalf of Mumia Abu-Jamal, the death row inmate from Philadelphia, Pennsylvania, who many are convinced is innocent of the crime he is charged with. Like so many others who have taken a stand against oppression, one way or another, the system finds a way to come down on you to the degree even your own people will, more often than not, side with the criminal system. People from around the world know this brother is not guilty. But few in the African-American community will take a stand on his behalf. Not so with the brother standing at the microphone, poised to recite his own poetry, dedicated to the freedom of Mumia Abu-Jamal, and revolution to free all political prisoners.

What immediately came to my mind, when he was reciting his first of three poems, was the poetry of the 60s, when the entire nation had the words of black poets "telling it like it was," each word dripping with the venom of having only words to fight with, against many years of having those in power act out their racism through the use of corrupt police and unjust laws. The black press always had space on their pages, to reflect the emotions of a people too long denied their human rights. The black press wrote about seeing son after son swinging from tree limbs with ropes around their necks, and snuffing out the lives of those whose only mistake was that of being "born in America as an Africans." Our poets told the world what it was like living in the wealthiest country on earth, with one of your sons swinging from the limb of a tree to remind you to "stay in your place" or the same thing could happen to you.

This is the picture he painted with the words he so artistically welded together. At the end of each poem the audience was on their feet; not only African-Americans but the whites, Hispanics, and Native Americans were all shouting their approval. He was good. I would have to say, he ranked right up near the top of the "street poets" that I had known from the 60s.

The Imam had done his homework on my background, had gotten information that only Brother Ali, the assistant co-founder of our organization, could have provided. He spoke briefly about my military background, about my family life, about my retirement as a postal employee, and the fact I had graduated from the California State University Dominguez Hills, Carson, California. While all of this may be impressive, it gave no clue as to why I was there. That I would have to convey in the time I was allotted.

I decided to speak on the subject, "African, Know Thyself," in honor of the occasion. First, I addressed the reason why I was in a position to be invited to speak at this celebration of the history of the African-American. Then I stressed the value of knowing and honoring our history as a people. Through knowing ourselves, we are in a better position to shape our own destiny, in a position to see why the incarceration of the African in America is fast becoming the new slave ideology of the 21st century. Only this time, the African-American is assisting the growth of slavery behind prison walls.

Without knowing the greatness of the black man, from day one to the present, great numbers of our males fall into the hands of the new slave makers. We cannot say we love and respect our great leaders, while daily breaking laws we know are passed for the purpose of increasing our numbers behind bars.

I spoke about the period when we came off the plantations, after the civil war, released, but far from being free. We had nothing but our spirits to sustain us. We should know we lived through a period of slavery unlike anything the world had ever witnessed before, took every beastly deed the slave owner heaped upon our heads, and still continued to stand tall as a people.

Many of our people died for trying to learn how to read. Now in the 21st century, many of our people are looking for ways to keep from learning to read and write. There is no way to escape having to come face to face with the reality of being an African, if Africa is your motherland. The people in a position of power will not let the African forget he is black, no matter how hard the African may try to forget it.

It is important that we understand many of our people died during the period of slavery, because they wanted to remain what the Creator had made them, Africans. In something less than two hundred years, all of our collective honor as an African people is falling by the wayside, for the lack of a committed effort to know ourselves as an African people willing to stand up for justice.

I informed the audience that my being there before them had to do with my total commitment to the Afrocentric education of those brothers, and sisters who are locked down behind prison walls—those African-American inmates that truly seek change in their lives, those who understand the black man, like his forefathers of yesterday, is faced with a war that is as devastating as anything we faced in the slave era. Not only does this war present enemies from without, it pits brother against brother, father against son, daughter against mother, within many homes throughout black America.

"Black on black crime takes a high toll among our people, with far too many black people being incarcerated, or going to an early grave. In many cases, drugs are found in abundance where miseducation of black people is paramount, where unemployment is high, where police oppression is available 24-7, 365 days, and there are guns in the hands of many who have not yet learned to value living.

"There must be men among the many that are incarcerated that truly wish to gain knowledge of the greatness of the African. It is for this purpose that I accepted the invitation to appear before you today to give you the opportunity to understand why the study of our history is not just a one-month affair. One could study the history of the African each day of his life, and still there would be more to study at the end of that life, which is a testimony to the greatness of the African's contribution to the vast body, known as world knowledge, or the history of mankind."

I extended an invitation to any inmate that truly wished to study the history of the African-Americans for the purpose of joining our team to fight ignorance on all fronts, to write to our organization requesting an enrollment form. We also have an idea to organize study groups inside prisons that seek such services. It was important that I paint a picture with words, a picture to inspire their dedication and commitment to the desire for a life other than incarceration. Working together, brothers inside with brothers outside, would make this idea possible.

Fortunately, seated in the audience were several members of the

Nation of Islam, who were very much interested in what I was saying. Say what you will about those within the Nation of Islam, they are one of the most dedicated groups towards the uplifting of Africans born in America, than any group, no matter their ideology.

Primarily, the followers of the Nation of Islam accepted my word, and worked with the Imam to bring about our first on-site study group, dealing with the understanding of Afrocentricity for individual growth and collective development.

Chapter 3

THE JOY OF KNOWING THYSELF

I have had it stated to me far too many times that, "Blacks should know their history." Seldom have I had it stated to me, "Blacks must commit to learning their history." Many hours have been invested in trying to arrive at a comfortable solution to this constant annoyance. Why? Why are blacks giving themselves a failing grade in this area?

Fear is playing a big role in holding blacks in a state of ignorance, when it comes to committing to learning their history—fear of inviting the pain of slavery into minds that would rather reject the

FROM MISEDUCATION TO INCARCERATION

truth, and never know the true joy of the greatness in 'knowing thyself.' While this is true how can we move forward in promoting awareness of the history of the African born in America?

Strangely enough, I came to realize the answer was within me, standing in my mind like some tormented slave that is repeatedly beaten down, only to rise up for another beating because he could not stay down, as long as there was strength enough in his body.

Each time I looked back into my memory, to the times whites had attempted to impress me with their knowledge of what they knew of my history, the answer was standing right there. I was being told a lie, and could feel it was a lie, but I was in no position to counteract the lie. Because at that point in my life, no black scholar had given me the historical information that I needed.

At those times in my life, I hadn't even bought a one-way ticket on "Tubman's Underground Railroad." Not yet come eye to eye with W.E.B. DuBois in his "Souls of Black Folks." I didn't know of his greatness, of his truth. I desperately needed to know these things in order to dispel these vicious lies, often used to dehumanize me. It was not always whites who used these lies, sometimes it was the negroes themselves that were terrified at the thought of "blackness."

These are the times when you need your scholars present, grounded tightly in your mind, leaving no room for racist white lies, or ignorant, negro lack of guts.

Negroes are made in America, in a racist European pattern, evolved from the minds of white Christians, concerned with building white wealth, and to hell with saving black souls. This has been the model since day one, building on the strong black backs of the African, while holding him in a state of continuing servitude, at the feet of another's greed.

What does knowing these truths do for me? It alerts me to the

THE JOY OF KNOWING THY SELF

fact, it is necessary for me to arm myself for the task ahead, a task as arduous as anything I have encountered thus far, in a life that has exposed me to walking among many different people on this planet. I now know from my experience, black people will never change their condition, without an individual commitment to change that brings forward a collective will of the majority. Nowhere I have traveled, have I ever found another people who were fearful of their own history.

My individual commitment to myself is to find the key to unlock this fear among the African born in American, and locked down in one of America's systems of wealth making, known as the "prison industrial complex."

It cannot be denied the African community in America needs a plan that teaches the history, that is so feared by so many who continue to exist in a pit of darkness. Deep in the souls of black people are scars of longing for something, something perhaps not yet known to the one who longs for it. One can go many years, and not identify the source of this longing.

I looked many places outside my mind, trying to get a hold of this elusive shadow that always seemed to stand just outside of my reality, stepping aside just when I had it within my grasp, leaving my mind in shambles each time. To keep denying that I needed help, would only delay filling the void in my psyche, which had been empty far too long.

First, I came through the Middle Passage with Lerone Bennett, Jr., in his text, "Before the Mayflower." I felt a sense of fulfillment I had never felt after reading the "Bible." Bennett was not telling me about the life and times of Jewish people, he put it on the line for me, giving me the words about my story. Not that the story of others is not important, it's just that my story is the one that is most important to me. After living inside the covers of Bennett's text for more than a few days, I knew there was even greater excitement awaiting me, along the highway leading to a more grounded Afrocentric education.

It was Richard Wright, the author of "Black Boy," who gave me a deep sense of pride in this masterfully written text. Knowing that there were writers the likes of Richard Wright gave me the opportunity to tell my children, they too could be a Richard Wright.

When the door of ignorance is left standing ajar, after the strength of "Black Studies" has moved against this barrier of racist denial, many wonderful things can happen by pushing the door completely open, making it possible for the works of other black scholars, to find their way into lives desperately in need of true Afrocentric knowledge.

Standing beside Ralph Ellison, understanding the plight of his "Invisible Man," brought into focus many questions that had long plagued my thoughts. Writers like Ralph Ellison, Frantz Fanon, James Baldwin, Richard Wright, and Claude Brown, each in his own words gave me inspiration, that to this day still accompanies me along the road to full knowledge, of who I am as an African born in America.

Afrocentric knowledge, even in small increments, can start an instant cure for the cancerous condition that seeks to deny the fact, "It would be better to be dead in Afrocentric hell, than to be a live negro spirit in some white heaven." If you truly understand you have the right to name yourself, think for yourself, and most of all, be yourself, then you must also know, beyond a shadow of a doubt, you have the right of your Creator, to name your own "HEAVEN AND HELL."

This is primarily the reason why the "haves" don't want the "have-nots" to become Afrocentrically informed. The truth will drive black people into a mindset that will fight for change in their realties.

These truths makes it imperative that our African-American inmates, those that want this knowledge in order to change the direction of their lives, move in the opposite direction away from crime. The prison system is not concerned with helping inmates turn their lives around. Nor are the state governments interested in keeping inmates from returning to their prisons. Because prison business is a sure way of amassing large amounts of money. Those who are instrumental in having state laws passed, like "California's three strikes law," to keep the prison cells filled to capacity, are only interested in how much they can increase their wealth, and not in rehabilitation.

Our plan is to bring the scholar to the inmate, through the teachings of Afrocentricity, using curriculums developed for outreach through the mails. It works very well, when all of the participants understand their roles.

Once an inmate is recruited into the program, he/she receives series of letters informing him/her about the mission of NABSIO, to spread Afrocentric knowledge throughout the prison industrial complex. It is no secret mission bound up in hatred, it is a proud moment that says, "To hell with a world, or system, that would deny me the opportunity to know myself, and indeed my history."

For once, it teaches the African-American inmate that he can stand, side by side, with his fellow inmates and say, "I wish to join with you in opening a new chapter in America's new method of enslaving the African-American, behind prison bars." If it is not slavery, then why isn't America using this time to educate the black people behind bars? (Ref. 13th amendment to the U.S. Constitution).

Knowing the hearts of America's "haves" we cannot stand idly by, thinking white America will one day change its mind about the status of the black community. Nor can we say that every inmate should not be behind bars, because he/she is black. Many inmates have done more to destroy the black community, than any other ethnic group. However, this should not, no matter the deed, stop any inmate from joining this movement to study his/her history. After all, it is their history, as well as, the history of all other members of the black community.

Once the inmate becomes a student in the NASBIO Afrocentric Program, it is then important to spread the word about how it is possible to learn the history of the African, to gain knowledge of self, while serving out a sentence.

Afrocentric knowledge is worth fighting for, worth standing up for, worth coming face to face with the fact we make life that much harder to live, when the courage is absent in the heart. Without the self-esteem gained through knowledge of self, the African-American inmate will always find it hard to understand why it is important to fight against unjust laws, like three strikes.

This is a war to free our minds from seeing ourselves as less than full citizens, in a nation where so much of the blood of our people has enriched the soil, drop after precious drop, from bodies broken by the forces of evil that hold the African in a continuous state of terror. Our unwillingness to engage in committed study, to at once know ourselves, gives support to keeping black Americans in a state of servitude, which makes it harder for the few who are willing to struggle against this form of slavery.

Know this fact, NABSIO does have a plan of national scope, created for the explicit purpose of Afrocentrically educating the black American inmate, without exception. Knowing yourself extends your ability in understanding you were not created to be a slave. You were not created to work for anyone. Your labor is a gift from your Creator, for you to apply to your needs, not to make others wealthy, at your own expense.

THE JOY OF KNOWING THY SELF

It is very important that the inmate student, at all times, knows that knowledge should always be used for the betterment of himself/herself, in building a stronger family and community. Our aim is to prove your incarceration should not determine the cessation of your service to your community, nor should it stop your growth academically. There are many reasons why the powers that be will not lift a helping hand to increase the level of Afrocentric knowledge throughout black America. A people who know themselves, also know when they are being exploited, and most importantly who is doing the exploiting.

Afrocentricity calls for the student to understand, it is the absence of knowledge, the unwillingness to study, to know yourself, to know you have a great purpose for being on this planet, that keeps your mind in bondage. Afrocentric knowledge leads the black mind to freedom, and away from racist lies, put there by years of oppression.

Once the African-American inmate realizes he/she can increase their value to the community, by doing intensive study in the field of Afrocentricity, the number of teachers will increase. Then, we can make a run against the level of psychological slavery, that holds black people in a state of economic poverty.

Our scholars have written the true story of the black American. Now, it is time for black America to learn this history, to push forward to true freedom. One may say he/she wants to be free, and still be unwilling to pay the price of freedom. Knowledge is the key. The inmate that understands this truth, and is willing to put himself/herself in the path of this runaway Afrocentric knowledge train, can change her entire mindset from slavery to freedom.

FROM MISEDUCATION TO INCARCERATION

To leave the consciousness of a "slave mentality" behind is an arduous process. Our scholars are here to help us do just that. No doubt, slavery damaged the ability of blacks to view themselves in the light of prior greatness, making it more difficult to eliminate inappropriate behavior toward each other. Evidence of this behavior is found in the teachings of Dr. Na'im Akbar's, "Breaking the Chains of Psychological Slavery," "The very nature of the slave's mentality insures that the majority of the slaves will be primarily committed to their master and his consciousness."

The NABSIO Education Plan recognizes the urgency of getting Dr. Akbar to occupy a seat at the planning table to mentally change prisons into universities. Again, not an easy process.

This opportunity must not pass by without the proper response from the community. A large segment of black America are in the criminal justice system, with no significant input from the black community, unless, you wish to count the number of black Americans that sleep in prison beds each night, as an input.

What this says is, the black American is not now committed to himself, nor committed to his/her ancestors, who already paid the price for the black American's freedom. To truly be aware of this reality, is to automatically be willing to make Afrocentric education a reality. In his book, "The Falsification of African Consciousness," Amos N. Wilson says, "If our education is not about gaining real power, we are being miseducated and misled and we will die 'educated' and misled."

The NABSIO Plan is a war plan that says to the families of incarcerated African-Americans, "Get involved, join your family member in this revolutionary education plan, lifting the 'power fist' strongly against apathy, and fear of commitment to work for change within the prison industrial complex."

THE JOY OF KNOWING THY SELF

This plan says to the African-American inmate, "Here is a gift of knowledge, something you can bring home when you leave the bars of horror, an Afrocentric education obtained while being locked down." You will be coming home conditioned to take your position in the ranks, seeking change in the African-American community.

There is something horrific about the way the black man lives his life, here in America. We clearly see the problems we face as a people, yet, making a collective effort to solve these problems seems to escape the majority of black Americans.

When we stop to observe the progress other groups are making, progress right in our own communities, we stand in admiration. Afrocentricity teaches, we need to understand the other people that come among us did not come with pockets filled with money. Our government, our tax dollars helped to make it possible for them to be successful. Once they apply for a business loan, and the bank grants the loan, their success is well on the way. Not because they are any greater at running a business, or that they have any greater degree of smarts than we do—no, that is not the case. When we look closer at this picture, we can see we hold the key to their success. Any time you walk by a business run by a black businessman, to spend your money with a non-black business in the black community, who run home after dark, with your money in a bag, the life blood of your community is contained in that bag. At the same time, the black businessman is still in his shop, hoping that some of the late business will come in his door. The other shop owner is somewhere in his own America, counting your money that he will place in his bank, two blocks from where he lives. Each dollar you spend in his nail, hair, and fast food business, is one more nail being driven into the heart of black America.

Many of the challenges the African in America face is a direct result of his unwillingness to get involved with the black man's history. We cannot overcome our struggle if we continue to refuse to know our own history, and to tie this history to our economic needs as a people.

Who is to take the leadership role in proving to the people that there is another way out of this hell? If it is not you, black inmate, then who? You are the one with the courage to spread the evil known as drugs, throughout black America, to its detriment. If you have the balls to kill your brother, over drugs that are given to you to kill your people, then where are your balls once you are locked down? Are they left at the prison door when you check in? You cannot have it both ways—selling drugs to make money for your own personal gain, while helping racism to harm your people. To do this, is a state of madness. You cannot lead our people with blinders on.

To remove these blinders, the African must "know himself" before he can lead anyone, anywhere. NABSIO's Plan is to educate those behind prison walls, throughout America's prison industrial complex. Don't look to find some preacher, or teacher, to clean up the damage caused by selling drugs throughout black America: the challenge stands before you, the inmate, the ex-offender, and yes, the black man standing on the sidelines, waiting for someone else to accomplish this job.

Brothers, sisters, we are in a war.

Chapter 4

FINDING AFROCENTRIC EDUCATION

Reality time. Knowing what you can do, and setting out to get it done. Developing a plan to provide funds for the purpose of financing, and procuring all necessary materials in building a reliable Afrocentric curriculum to educate African-American inmates is a must.

Money! Always the one element that often prevents the African-American from working out solutions, that have long been known to be advantageous for the welfare of blacks. Ideas die on the planning

FROM MISEDUCATION TO INCARCERATION

table, for lack of money. Thus, finding a way to make it possible to put into operation a sound program that can gain the respect of African-Americans in prison was no easy task.

Throughout the Third World, nation after nation work through their problems without a great deal of money. Only in the Western nations is money given such a high success, or failure rating, when seeking to implement a new plan.

The National Association of Brothers and Sisters In & Out (NABSIO), has stayed alive, going in and out of prisons throughout the state of California, without any funds. Not that funds were not needed. Funds were not available to buy books written by black scholars, for the purpose of educating black inmates. No, you won't find any money handy to pay for this kind of education. Over the past ten years, our organization worked hard to develop a plan, through trial and error, whereby Afrocentric education can be brought to black Americans behind bars, at minimum cost.

The need to educate our people in prison, is a problem for all black Americans. Therefore, we needed a financial plan that would make it possible to spread the cost throughout black America.

The plan fell into place, following the Million Man March, after it was suggested that those at the march could return home and adopt a brother or sister behind bars, for the purpose of bonding with them, in order to assist in finding ways to bring them back to a better way of life. The Honorable Minister Louis Farrakhan of the Nation of Islam, one of black America's best-beloved sons, made this wonderful suggestion. It didn't happen, no matter how hard some of the marchers wanted to see it come about. Still, NABSIO persisted until there was a workable plan available, for any inmate that wanted to enroll in the NABISO program for the betterment of self.

Some months prior to the date of the Million Man March, our

organization was already developing a sponsorship program, not much different from our present program, known as NABSIO's Adopt A Prisoner. In theory the two concepts drew their energy from the same source.

The black American is at a considerable disadvantage, from the first instant he appears before a judge. That is just one of many problems blacks must contend with behind bars. The biggest problem is the problem of illiteracy. Some researchers place the rate of prison illiteracy as high as 70 percent throughout the United States. With half the prison population coming from the community being comprised of black Americans, it is safe to say over 70 percent of this population is illiterate.

There are few, if any, politicians, black or white, willing to address this problem. This number reflects the inferiority of our education system, that this percent of Americans have fallen through the cracks. NABSIO not only talks about this problem, it seeks to unite families of inmates and ex-offenders to support their loved ones, by getting involved with a community-based program to combat this injustice.

Writing about this problem, talking about this injustice, without taking action, or at least having the courage to put a plan into operation, that can move against the apathy which eats away at the very collective will of black people—this, too, is an injustice.

The genius of this plan is its simplicity. It calls for black scholars to go to prison, not in the physical sense, but the literary sense. In this way all scholars are available to come to our assistance, to enter each prison where there are inmates enrolled as students. Their concepts and ideas on Afrocentricity can enter the minds of blacks behind prison walls, in a way never before imagined.

It has always been known by our staff, even before our plan was

FROM MISEDUCATION TO INCARCERATION

finalized, that our scholars were the key to teaching Afrocentricity. In Dr. Na'im Akbar's, "Visions for black Men," he makes it plain what the black inmate should be doing, while locked behind prison bars. He tells us, he is "...confident that if these confined men want freedom they must free their minds and start not being 'prisoners' and start redefining what their situation is." How will the multitude of black inmates ever read these words, if the works of Dr. Akbar and other black scholars don't come into their hands? This is now within reach. All that is required are committed student inmates, and committed sponsors nationwide.

Without a committed public to individually, and collectively, sponsor our enrolled students, the plan is made more difficult. Not impossible, just more difficult. This clearly shows why it is so important, that family and friends understand the role they are to fill in insuring the success of this financial plan. They can sponsor an inmate by being willing to accept the responsibility of paying for an inmate student's textbooks. In the case of a relative that is incarcerated, if you wish to encourage their enrollment in NABSIO's Afrocentric Education program, all that is required is to contact the main office of this program. All information about the sponsor is confidential, even from our inmate students who are being sponsored by a relative, as a matter of policy.

Once the sponsor is registered, and a student inmate is identified and enrolled, the process starts. First, a letter is sent to the inmate providing information about NABSIO, and its mission. A pre-enrollment exam, composed of fifty multiple-choice Afrocentric questions, will indicate how much the student already knows, concerning his/her history. After the results of this exam is known, the first textbook, "Lessons From History: A Celebration In Blackness," by Dr. Jawanza Kunjufu, is sent to the inmate student, with a study guide to assist the student to get the most from this text. The cost to the sponsor for this first text is fourteen dollars; that covers the cost of the textbook, handling, and mailing.

It is important to state at this point, that this same program is available to the sponsor, or any younger family members. With more than one member of a family taking the course, the reward is greatly magnified.

Following the policy of our organization, the sponsors are encouraged to correspond with the student being sponsored, to assist in their development. However, when corresponding, a mailing system should be established for the purpose of security and protection. Our program assumes no responsibility for the release of addresses, phone numbers, or other vital information. Sponsors should remain objective in encouraging self-development, and resist becoming emotionally attached through correspondence.

After the completion of each text and assignments, the sponsor will be notified that the student is ready to continue their studies with the next book. This process will be repeated with each text until the course is completed. When the course is completed, the student will receive a certificate of completion. However, it must be understood that the course is not accredited. All student inmates, upon release, are encouraged to continue their training, by enrolling in some training development program.

Funding a large scale education program is always possible when the cost is evenly spread throughout the total population interested in the program. Each sponsor is requested to assist in helping to get the word out to church members, fellow social groups, clubs, and others, about reaching out to our people behind bars.

When our numbers are great enough, the possibility exists of creating online products to market throughout black America to raise

FROM MISEDUCATION TO INCARCERATION

more funds for expanding this education program. We must do something about functional illiteracy. The problem is much too large for the black community to behave as if it doesn't exist.

Even while we seek ways to fund educating black inmates, others are seeking ways to increase the number of blacks in prison, making it all the more important for black people to evolve in ways to take care of ourselves.

There's no leadership coming out of Washington, D.C., showing ways to lower the number of black people in prison. However, there are leaders in Washington, sending out information expressing that they feel that the present laws are not harsh enough for anyone that is caught in the drug madness. Those that fund the U.S. Drug War, and push this nation in the direction of a snitch culture, are not the people who favor education.

As cruel as this behavior is towards the oppressed people in America, it is far more harmful to feel powerless, to the point of doing nothing to help yourself. Education is a weapon, and knowledge can be a crusade to free one's spirit. Each member of a family should be willing to make sure all family members obtain as much education as is possible for that family.

Always, at what cost? How many inmates are willing to pay for their own textbooks? This answer will come later, as will many other answers beneficial to the welfare of black America. Just to know there are African-American inmates willing to pay for our program, to educate themselves, is very encouraging for our future.

Having to step forward and pay for our education isn't a new phenomenon for the African-American. Dr. Claud Anderson, founder and president of The Harvest Institute, a think-tank whose mission is the social and economic reform of black America, tells us, "When schools were finally built…blacks were forced to finance their own schools and pay tuition to non-black schools."

FINDING AFROCENTRIC EDUCATION

At this point, it is important to note the need for the black woman to understand this Afrocentric program. First of all, the black woman is the real strength behind what little education the black child receives in America. To understand that she is a force to be reckoned with, one only has to examine the American black church. This strength comes in the form of money. It is the black women who basically finance the black church through tithes and fundraising events.

Haki R. Madhubuti, author of "Black Men: Obsolete, Single, Dangerous?" made the following observations. "It is the black woman that far outnumbers the black male. The black church would not exist as such a force if it were not for black women who have, by and large, financed 'modern' black churches."

Many of these same dedicated churchwomen are the mothers of many of the black inmates locked down in America's prisons. Thus, it is important that they understand, with their support, a change can occur behind prison walls. It is a fact, the white leadership in America is using the prison industrial complex to provide a place for a large percentage of disillusioned black males. Madhubuti says, "The U.S. white supremacy system works overtime to disrupt black men... The most prevalent tactics used are...: Use the prison system as a breeding ground for hard, non-political black men who, for the most part, will return and prey on their own communities. (There are exceptions.)"

This is the information the black community needs to know. There are many criminal-minded blacks and there are those that seem to oppose positive change. For them, behind the walls of America's prisons, is, perhaps, the very best place for them.

With the families of presently locked-down blacks, and the families of ex-offenders, working with our women inside the churches throughout black America, a change will come. There is a need to create opportunities for those individuals, coming home from the system, who need employment. No agency in sight, black or white, is overly concerned with assisting the black ex-offender to find a better life, making it all the more important for us, to step up to the plate and demand to become a player in this game of life. We must overcome the fear factor that keeps so many African-Americans standing on the sidelines, when their participation in the game of life is so greatly needed.

As stated earlier in this chapter, our plan is not complicated. It draws upon the teachings of leaders such as Marcus Garvey and Elijah Muhammad, who clearly define the importance of education. However, it is the words of Elijah Muhammad which have the greatest meaning for our purpose.

> My people should get an education which will benefit their own people and not an education adding to the "storehouse" of their teacher. We need education, but an education which removes us from the shackles of slavery and servitude. Get an education, but not an education which leaves us in an inferior position and without a future. Get an education, but not an education that leaves us looking to the slave master for a job.

Similar teachings of Elijah Muhammad are also found in Dr. Na'im Akar's book, "Know Thyself."

Chapter 5

DANIELLE AND THE DEA

The inspiration for this chapter came from a conversation I had with a young inmate, at the Terminal Island Federal Facility for men, a year or so before this inmate won his release.

At the time of our first meeting, he was certain he would spend the next twenty years in prison. Fortunately for him, there were those on the outside working to bring him home earlier. They eventually succeeded.

We were not aware he had received an early release, but on a visit to one of the sites where we were seeking a sponsorship connection,

FROM MISEDUCATION TO INCARCERATION

he was there, working. Full of brotherly joy at the sight of his two former cultural mentors, he told us all about his release, and we explained all that we had accomplished since we had last met. He told us there was something he felt we should know.

The information he gave me concerned the incarceration of a young African-American female, being held at the Federal Facility for Women, in Northern California. The more he told us the angrier I became. Just the idea that our Criminal Justice Department, can, and often does, send our citizens to prison with sentences so horrific, it should sicken any fair-minded human being, as it did me.

I knew I had to tell Danielle's story, and how racist drug agents can harm poor families without any sense of fairness or accountability to anyone.

I rented a car from a dealer on Aviation Boulevard, near the Airport in Los Angeles, California, for a trip to the Oakland area where Dublin Federal Prison for Women is located.

The drive up, like so many others I've taken, started at midnight. It was a clear night, with traffic flowing very smoothly, making it possible to get out of the Los Angeles metropolitan area without difficulty.

As I passed Six Flags Magic Mountain, the lights on some of the rides were still pushing back the darkness as I continued on my way into the Grapevine, on I-5 Freeway North. I figured I would make good time, if I didn't run into any accidents.

I made good time, in spite of the light rain that was falling just north of Fresno, which increased slightly for the last hundred miles. Since I was early by an hour or more, I pulled into an AM/PM gas stop to kill a few minutes before continuing on my journey to Dublin.

What would I find at Dublin? Would Danielle understand the purpose of a man in his early seventies driving this distance alone, to visit a female inmate he had never met? Even though we had exchanged several letters, after being introduced by a young man I had met at a male federal prison, at San Pedro, California, this trip would bring me face to face for the first time with an individual to whom the court in New Orleans had given the severest sentence I had ever heard of.

The rain was still falling ever so lightly, as I turned on to the Dublin off ramp. Some ten minutes later I drove into the prison parking area. Not knowing if there were facilities inside, where I could change into my Afrocentric attire, I elected to use the privacy of my car.

Wanting to make a strong impression on Danielle, I had selected the most African-looking suit that I owned. I was reassured when the white guard, working the front desk, gave me a warm compliment on my apparel.

Locating my name on the visiting log, I discovered I was approved to enter the prison visiting area set aside for outside visitors. Clearing the metal detector, I was now ready to be escorted over to my rendezvous with Danielle.

I had no idea she would be nervous over meeting me for the first time. Being busy with my own thoughts, I had selfishly disregarded how she might feel, about meeting a stranger. Sure enough, her apprehension delayed our first meeting for some forty minutes. Several calls were placed over to the dormitory where Danielle lived, to make sure she was aware she had a visitor waiting in the visiting room.

Finally, she appeared in the doorway, coming through from the inmate entrance—a small exquisite female with very striking eyes that warmed your heart the moment you made eye contact. She didn't reach my shoulder in height, as I folded her into my arms and gave her a fatherly hug to put her at ease.

FROM MISEDUCATION TO INCARCERATION

Here we were, face to face at last. The first thing she wanted to know was how I made the trip up from Los Angeles. She was serving a prison sentence of three lifetimes, plus twenty years, and she was concerned about my safety. Right then I knew there was more to this very delicate spirit, and I was compelled to do all in my power to assist her in telling her story.

Who is Danielle Bernard-Metz? A mother of two wonderful children, that the federal government felt didn't need their mother for the next three lifetimes, plus twenty years. Where justice walked out of the courtroom, the miscarriage of justice walked in wearing a black robe, and took a seat on the bench in order to let the game begin. In the courtroom (slave block), Danielle was now in a position to learn what many African-Americans learn early in life—the white male Americans make the laws, and break the laws whenever it suits them, which has little or nothing to do with justice. Danielle would soon learn that the majority of judges are nothing more than henchmen for the new slavocracy, the prison industrial slave system.

The white male, for many years, has lynched, bombed, raped, murdered, assassinated, and framed African-American people, from the time the two people first came in contact with each other, until the present. Had Danielle been taught the true history of our people, she would have known white judges and white juries are not about justice the moment she was led into the courtroom. They sit in these jury boxes knowing full well that lies are being used by the majority of today's prosecutors, and it makes no difference, just as long as the defendant is a black man, or woman.

More than anything, Danielle wants other young women to know, if you are in a relationship and think something of a criminal nature may be taking place, run, don't walk, to the nearest exit and keep going. Don't even think about looking back.

DANIELLE AND THE SEA

Danielle is a fighter with much to fight for, as she serves her sentence in Dublin Federal Facility for Women. Her crime—if you can label her unwillingness to bear false witness against her husband, at the command of a corrupt federal official working as a DEA agent—a crime, then you can say Danielle is charged with a crime. Until the courts rids itself of white supremacy and racism, the Danielles of America should not be surprised when they receive something other than "justice."

The Danielle I met was greatly concerned that many unwary young women, like herself, think America is a free society for all its citizens. Not so. Many are under the delusion that if they are arrested and charged with some crime, they will receive fair treatment under the justice system. They disregard those few voices throughout the African-American community, calling for our youth to beware of the government's "war" on drugs, which is nothing more than a guise to cover her greed, in order to support her growing prison industrial slave system.

To those Africans born in America, still living in some utopian dream world, who truly believe the slavocracy in this country is a thing of the past, should not call "Tyrone" they should call Danielle. Ask her to tell you about the "Thirteenth Amendment" to the Constitution, which states:

> Neither Slavery nor involuntary Servitude, Except for Punishment of a Crime, where the party shall be Duly Convicted shall exist in these United States or any place under its Jurisdiction.

Demonizing an innocent party makes it easier for the public to accept any punishment handed out by the courts; they think nothing of giving a Danielle three life terms plus twenty years. This decision comes from the white males on the bench, working hand in hand, with the same motives that drove their forefathers to plunder, murder, rape, and enslave an entire continent, all for the sake of power-driven capitalist greed. They give out long unreasonable prison sentences, which keep the prison industrial slave system overpopulated in all the states where there are large numbers of African-Americans and other low income citizens living.

Danielle has a human right to question what degree of sentence should be imposed upon an individual apprehended, not with five kilograms of imaginary cocaine, but trying to bring a speedboat filled with drugs into the country—drugs that weigh hundreds of pounds.

You can find the answer to questions of this kind when you understand slaves own very few speedboats in America. Therefore, the power-driven greed mongrels make sure the unjust courts and the corrupt drug agents hand out the severest punishment for conspiracy to sell drugs to the poor and legally defenseless.

Not only does the conspiracy law provide drug agents the opportunity to frame innocent victims, it also makes it possible for these same agents to cause severe damage within the immediate families of their victims.

The agent has the power to offer a known criminal a much lighter sentence to give false testimony against someone a corrupt drug agent has decided to entrap—in this case, Danielle. She had the courage to stand up to a DEA agent, and refuse to give false testimony against another person—her husband. If you think this cannot happen to you, again I invite you to ask "Danielle."

It takes a certain kind of courage that comes from deep within, perhaps from the very depths of our spirits, from the "will" developed by our foreparents as they lived the experience of plantation existence to display this kind of resistance. There are cases in the history of the African slave in this country, where the slave owner would use this same method of dealing with slave families. Pit one member against another for the purpose of instilling fear in order to control.

The hour is late, the black man and woman are no longer needed in the society we have come to know as a Christian way of life. How far should we trust a Christian society that will stand idly by and witness this build-up of slave genocide against the same people that never fully departed the tentacles of early American slavery?

So, what is being said here, is all of this talk about the tremendous increase in putting citizens in prison for nonviolent crimes, is viewed as a way to put the most rebellious behind bars, as a way to keep unemployment figures from casting a negative light on the big "lie." The Wall Street Journal reported (Feb.1, 2000): "Prisoners are excluded from employment calculations. And since most inmates are economically disadvantaged and unskilled, jailing so many people has effectively taken a big block of the nation's least-employable citizens out of the equation." Just give them long-term sentences, where they are made slaves for life, supporting, and working for the rich and greedy.

This publication is not looking to change the minds of capitalist power brokers on Wall Street. Our purpose is to convince the Danielles throughout America, who at this time have not fallen into the quicksand pits, camouflaged by the Clinton Administration's sugar-coated Drug Enforcement Administration, the number one slave maker, in the name of "war on drugs." Although the Clinton Administration will not put it in writing, it is well understood among African-American activists, that putting large numbers of blacks in prison is "good for the country." If good can be viewed as increased stock value, and the country can be looked upon as the power elite in

America, then by all means large numbers of blacks in prison are good for the country.

Some see the criminalization of women as a growing problem that has come to the attention of the Third National Conference of African-American Women that recently met in Washington, D.C. Lawyers from all across this nation were inspired to gather for the purpose of addressing this growing problem.

The conference reported in The Final Call newspaper (May 30, 2000): "The war on drugs is the single most important factor in the rise of incarcerated women. It has discriminated against black women using drugs and those not using drugs," according to Angela J. Davis, professor at American University's Washington College of Law.

In this same issue, Nisa Islam Muhammad, Staff Writer, depicted the case of Kemba Smith. This case has received national prominence, and rightly so. At the tender age of 23, Kemba fell into the pit of quicksand and was given 24.5 years behind bars, although she had no prior record. Again, the male enters the picture as a drug dealer, and the law went after the girlfriend, as women advocates at the conference testified.

Look at the parallel between Kemba Smith's case, and Danielle Metzs,' the DEA agent came after Danielle, because of her husband's supposed drug dealing. In both cases we see young African-American females, right in the middle of America's vicious and racist war on drugs, which is as devastating to the African-American family as anything I witnessed in the streets of Saigon, during the Vietnam War. Kemba Smith's case of 24.5 years pales by comparison, when held up to the light of injustice, found in the three life terms plus twenty years of Danielle's case. Not that Kemba's case is less horrendous, it indicates the injustice found in the drug laws of this nation, when the African-American is standing before the judges of this drug-infested society.

The Kemba Smiths and Danielle Metzs must also do their part to help pull other young females back from the brink of destruction. This story must be told on Sunday from the pulpit, on Monday from the garbage pit, on Tuesday from the snake pits of America's illegal drug industry.

The message coming from our young women, the Danielles and Kembas, must be that there's no penis ever born of woman, no matter how many thousand dollar bills its wrapped in, worth a lifetime of slavery in some prison hellhole. These boyfriends are devoid of any semblance of a conscience, these husbands have no sense of family, or people pride, nor an awareness of a higher spiritual force, that would prevent them from pulling their mates into the evil clutches of today's slave lords. Without the illegal behavior of thoughtless black males, ruthless drug agents would not have an opportunity to display their narcissistic nature, in relationship to black Americans. In short, many black people are aiding and abetting the enemy of African-Americans.

Anytime a black man sells drugs, robs and kills other black people, he is hurting the collective cause that moves black people forward. The police on the streets, the lawyers in the courtroom, the D.A.s that are too happy to jail black men, the judges that wear the robes, are the ones against the African-American. It does not take the genius of Imhotep to figure out the solution to this equation. No matter which direction the black American turns, he finds obstacles in his path, obstacles that are not presented to any other ethnicity. Still, America just possibly might be the best of all possible worlds—although the final vote is not yet tallied on this issue.

Afrocentric reality is not a Barbie doll story, the African-

FROM MISEDUCATION TO INCARCERATION

American community grows its young girls up for survival of the African in America. These girls are not to be pawns in a genocidal sham called the "war on drugs." This is better understood when you examine how the prison population increased over the past decade.

First, there were a series of laws passed, laws that left no doubt who was the primary targeted group. All across America, states put laws on their books called "Three Strikes" and "Mandatory Minimums." These laws keep the state prisons filled to over-capacity, with non-violent offenders. In the majority of these cases the offenders are there for life.

The second racist manifestation of hatred is found at the federal level. Taking a page out of his own book on how not to treat human being, while serving as governor in 1973, Nelson Rockefeller pushed through laws making possession of 4 ounces of any illegal drug subject to a mandatory sentence of 15 years to life.

Here we are some 27 years later, and these same archaic laws are being used to keep the federal prison system expanding at a dangerous pace for the African-American, who finds himself unable to receive proper training on the outside of prison walls, but in great demand, when needed by UNICOR, the federal government's labor program, behind prison walls.

Danielle, like so many other victims of America's unwinnable war, and her family had to learn the hard way. Because many families at the lowest end of government have known for some time, America's "war on drugs" has little to do with putting drug kingpins behind bars. The families that no longer enjoy the laughter that once came easy, are now afflicted with pain, caused by the unjust sentencing of many minor drug offenders.

The African-American mother is long-suffering. She brought her people through slavery, with the courage and the strength found in her genes that withstood the holocaust of the Middle Passage—only to find a holocaust of a different hue, at journey's end. Like the Middle Passage, this new holocaust delivered pain to the African mother, as devastating as that of the Middle Passage. She was now faced with a holocaust "American style," slavery, in the new age.

This new holocaust that is wreaking havoc with many African-American families of today has paused at the threshold of the Bernard Family, and delivered a shocking miscarriage of justice to Danille Bernard-Metz of New Orleans, Louisiana, in the form of three life terms at the Dublin Federal Prison for Women. The Drug Enforcement Administration, this nation's newest slave-making agency, is sending the Danielle Metzs and the Kemba Smiths to prison, with evidence no just judge would authorize.

There are several points to be made by the African-American non-violent offender, caught up in America's lust for a system to provide a continuous flow of monies, with minimum investments, to the prison industrial complex. This same system was used by today's lawmaker's ancestors, in building the most horrendous slave system known to mankind, in America's South.

First, this nation no longer has use for the offspring of its first free labor source, the ancestors of today's Africans in America. To the African in America it is apparent that the sons of former slave owners, are imbued with an ever burning hatred for the sons of the former slaves. In order to display this hatred, a legal means is established to once more place the African at a disadvantage, while simultaneously filling their racist pockets to the top. They have put into operation an industry with unlimited growth potential—the American prison slave system. There is now a great need for the African's free labor, working behind prison walls.

The power brokers in America realized the potential, when the mandatory sentencing law was passed by Congress in 1986. This moved judicial sentencing discretion to federal prosecutors. From all available information, this slave making body, changed these laws without consultation from any of its supposed experts in the Drug Enforcement Agency, from the judges or the U.S. Sentencing Commission, or from the Bureau of Prisons. Why? Could it be the idea to bring slavery back with a "bang" was so overwhelming in racist potential, that once the other "good old boys" understood what was going on, they too would follow in step? Anything is possible where billions are to be made by dealing in human suffering, something the African in America is well acquainted with having lived under some of the most racist laws for the past four hundred years, that present laws, pales in comparison. These laws give the impression that they have evolved out of a deep sense of justice, when in reality, just the opposite is true. To the black living in America, whose historical awareness follows the line of reasoning advanced by Malcolm X, El Hajj Malik El Shabazz, "The black American will never receive true justice living in a subservient existence with whites."

It is the black FAMILY that is under attack. To know the history of black Americans is to understand the slave owners had no compassion for the slave family. No amount of tears could deter the slave owner's destruction of black families when the opportunity presented itself to add to their greedy coffers. Thus, when viewed through eyes that looked upon this same pattern during the American slave era, we can understand the unjust sentences given to the Danielles in this new threat placed at the very heart of today's black family.

There are families living within a few hundred miles where a relative is incarcerated, and do not have the means to visit more than one or two times a year. For economic reasons, low income families are again looking at a situation they have seen in the past.

In the case of the Bernard Family, not only are they faced with having a female behind bars, they have to contend with this member being over two thousand miles from their home, making it near impossible for the children to have any meaningful relationship with their mother. Wasn't this method introduced during the slave era? Breaking up families by selling off its members for profit, no matter how much pain and suffering it inflicted upon the slave family? By incarcerating the parents of a given number of children, for long periods of time, you can sell stock in building new prisons for the children that will be coming in the future to fill the new cells.

These children that are casualties of America's "drug war," are just as helpless as the children I witnessed in Korea and Vietnam during those wars. They are victims of man's greed, and desire for unlimited power cloaked in white supremacy. That is an attitude I found expressed in the words of a group of "prominent white citizens" of Tuskegee, Alabama, found in "The Black Mood," by Lerone Bennett, Jr., 1964, "You understand," the prominent white citizen said in 1923, "that we have the legislature, we make the laws, we have the judges, the sheriffs, the jails. We have the hardware stores and the arms." They are well aware of the harm done to the black family. For they do indeed have the power to make slaves, at whatever frequency their greed dictates. A further glimpse of Danielle Metz's story will help drive this point home.

Perhaps a clearer picture can be gotten from Danielle's own account of the case, in a paper she prepared to be read at a "Women's Conference" held at the University of Berkley, in 1998:

FROM MISEDUCATION TO INCARCERATION

A WOMAN'S STORY

by Danielle Metz

When I look in the mirror I do not see a criminal, or a threat to society. But when the judge in New Orleans sentenced me five years ago, he said that I had forfeited my right to live in a humane society. Sometimes in the middle of the night I awaken to those words.

At the age of 26, mother of two small children, I was sentenced along with my husband to three life sentences plus 20 years. It was my first offense and my first involvement with the law.

Our charge was conspiracy to distribute five kilograms of cocaine—cocaine that was never seen, never produced, never confiscated from any of the nine defendants in our case. No substantial evidence was presented at our trial, only hearsay. The government constructed their case on the testimony of people who were already in prison at the time of our trial. Each of the men who testified received generous reductions in their sentences. Some of them were serving sentences of about 30 years; now they are free. Some had even been caught with drugs. To make the case against us, the government was willing to do whatever they could to win. Two of my co-defendants had already been sentenced on the cocaine charges, yet the judge didn't rule on double jeopardy until after all of us had been convicted as well.

Before our trial, I had no idea what conspiracy was. I'd never heard of it. Until this case, I had had no contact with criminal law. At the time of my arrest, the agents told me that I was not the one they were after. They told me explicitly that I would go free if I "cooperated." I did testify at my trial, in my own behalf, because I didn't think

I stood a chance otherwise. I didn't realize that I never stood a chance at all. I just wouldn't "cooperate" enough to satisfy the prosecutors. I didn't even know enough information to use to buy my freedom if I had been willing to.

On the day the trial began, the prosecutor offered me a deal: 20 years. At the time 20 years sounded like life to me—especially for something I did not do. So I turned it down, unaware of how high the cards were stacked against me in the courtroom.

I was the only woman among all the defendants. By association, it seemed I was involved in the long list of criminal acts the witnesses described. By the time they were all done testifying, the five kilograms of cocaine in the indictment had grown to something like 80 tons—if you believed the witnesses, who were there to save their own lives. My attorney assured me that he had tried to get my case severed from the others, to avoid the guilt by association—the only guilt ascribed to me. But I learned that he had never filed for severance. After the conviction, I fired this attorney and asked for a court-appointed lawyer. The court turned around and appointed the very same lawyer. How could I raise the issue of ineffective assistance of counsel with the same gentleman representing me? My chance for winning my freedom on appeal was slim to none. Because I didn't know any better, I went along with all of it.

I am now 31 years old, five years later, still in prison fighting for my freedom. I was the first woman in New Orleans ever to be sentenced to this type of time for drugs or conspiracy to distribute drugs. This used to be shocking, unheard of, but it's becoming a fact of everyday life. I'm sure almost everyone at this conference has heard of the nightmare of Kemba Smith. Well, there are about 15,000 similar nightmares that go unheard of—women locked up for 15, 20, 30 years, or life, because of their relationship to a man (often an older

FROM MISEDUCATION TO INCARCERATION

man ...) Kemba is fortunate because she has parents who are go-getters, dedicated to winning her freedom. Most of the women in prison don't have anywhere near that kind of support. Most of us don't even have any legal help—we're left to try to figure out what the outdated law books in the prison library are talking about. I've been without an attorney for four years now, and I'm the rule, not the exception.

If you accept your time and settle in to try to improve your education in prison, you face obstacles as well—no more college courses, no scholarship funds for correspondence courses, and cruelest of all, I've met with a rule that bars anyone with a long sentence from some of the few courses that are offered.

But the hardest part of all is the separation from my children. We need each other terribly. How do you tell your child 'Mama will never be coming home?' My heart aches to know that all the love I pour out to them may not be enough to convince them that I haven't left them so far away out of not caring for them. This is not just my tragedy, not just my children's tragedy. It's a tragedy shared by women, children, families and communities across this country. Everywhere, kids are being deprived of mothers and fathers, leaving the kids to think they don't have a hope in the world. The laws and the 'legal' process that took me away from what the judge called "a humane society" are doing lasting damage to the society.

As of now, all I have is prayer that something will change with these unjust sentences. I refuse to think there's no way out!

Thank you for reading this. I hope you will think of ways to help change this situation that punishes young women for our relationship to men, and for being unable or unwilling—or—both to give information against our husbands, the fathers of our children.

DANIELLE AND THE SEA

Hotep!

This is not nearly the full story on Danielle's life. I am hopeful, one day she will give us a book that will help many other trusting young women, who have no idea what the "war on drugs" is really all about and how mandatory sentencing, has increased incarceration of the black female. America seems willing to return this nation to a legal slave system.

When the European first came to Africa he was an unknown quantity to its inhabitant. It didn't take him long to reveal his true demonic character. Many millions of African lives were lost. History bears witness to this barbaric behavior, that appears to delight in inflicting pain on defenseless victims, pain that continues to grow in intensity, as the years pass behind prison walls. All the players in this vicious game of life, the Drug Enforcement Administration, the Federal Bureau of Investigation, and all departments of police, both local and federal, are on the sidelines waiting to enter the game against the African-American, whenever called.

The pain of being incarcerated is unceasing. The pain of not being at home when your niece is killed in a fit of rage. Not being there to tell your daughter about life, and the things she needs to hear from her mother. Unable to tell your son you will always have his back, in times of need. Unable to be there to comfort your sister over the loss of her daughter. Not being able to hug this same sister who is now aunt and mother to her niece, your daughter. A sister who had to step up to the plate, in this game of life, to become mother, grandmother, aunt and love giver of children that found themselves in need of this love and protection. Oh yes, whether the Danielles of this nation's war on crime are guilty or innocent, it makes little difference to the system now pushing to enlarge the prison industrial complex on every turn.

As bleak as this picture is for Danielle, there is still hope. There is a movement underway to organize a strong Defense Committee, to forge a continuous effort to free Danielle and other African-American mothers taken out of the lives of their children by an uncaring system.

Chapter 6

DISAVOWING THE ADDICTION TO VIOLENCE AMONG AFRICAN-AMERICANS

We came to this land in a state of violence, we worked from sunup to sundown to build a foundation for this nation, without receiving one red cent, always under the threat of death, or bodily harm for minimal production, even though our labor came free to the oppressor. When the days of physical slavery were ended, the violence against the ex-slave accelerated, in order to stifle the move towards freedom on the part of the newly freed Africans.

The African-American must look to himself, to solve the weakness that brings us in contact with violence. There are many men

FROM MISEDUCATION TO INCARCERATION

and women among inmates, and ex-offenders from the black community, that no longer want to follow the path of violence. This is no idle chatter. This statement is based on years of onsite investigation, in and out of prisons, talking with many inmates that want a new life, a life free of crime and violence.

At no time is the black American, living in the inner city, in a position to say he or she is free of the threat of violence. And the threat comes not only from those that would break the law, sometimes it is those paid to protect you that pose the greatest danger. It seems they are themselves living in a state of fear, causing some of them to be even more dangerous than the criminals.

In this nation, non-profit organizations are in a position to seek protection, when going up against the power bloc of the government or the state. The black inmate, and ex-offender, must organize in order to help his or her own situation. There is much that can be accomplished by individuals who are determined to make a new life after years of being locked down.

In order to put together a defense fund and support system to protect ourselves while working to build a better life, we must come together. Now! As individuals we are weak, together we have strength to help our families.

We know there is no other ethnic group, standing beside the African-American, as he fights for a fair share of the American pie. Say what you will about the opportunities available in this nation, they are indeed few for the ex-offender. There were few before he became an offender; therefore, we cannot say this situation is any surprise.

If we apply our collective will to this problem, we can, without a doubt, bring about positive change in the lives of many ex-offenders and their families. All wars are not shooting ones. The one the black

American is trapped in, although not a shooting war, is still very deadly. Many black inmates and ex-offenders assisted the oppressors in placing African-American communities in the center of this present war zone, with their voluntary criminal behavior. The consciously aware black inmate and ex-offender know they must shoulder part of the blame for the black communities' violent problems.

There are a few concerned African-Americans, throughout this nation, reaching out to the black inmate, and ex-offender, saying, "we are here for you" but, there has to be a willingness on the part of each individual to stand up and be counted in curbing violence.

One of the organizations reaching out to the black inmate and ex-offender is the National Association of Brothers and Sisters In & Out (NABSIO). We are reaching out to build a brotherhood of ex-offenders, offering the foundation for a support system strong enough to combat violence, and other such weaknesses as functional illiteracy and cultural ignorance. This brotherhood must become self-sustaining, in order to gain independence from those who refuse employment to ex-offenders seeking positive change.

The previous Democratic system, under Clinton, did much to criminalize a large segment of the African-American community. There are statistics that indicate some 2 million individuals are behind bars, and another 4 or 5 million are on parole or probation. With America's current pattern of incarcerating more Africans than any other ethnicity, logic dictates that some 2.8-3 million parole or probation statistics represent blacks. For any individual that doubt these statistics, just do the math for yourself.

There is a sound probability that there are some 5-10 million African-American inmates, ex-offenders, families, friends, and other concerned individuals, impacted by this nation's prison industrial complex. In many cases the black community is victimized by the criminal justice system, that continues to place many of its citizens in the hands of the prison system. This behavior is not likely to change in the foreseeable future. Thus, an organization which focuses on education, within our communities, about the dangers of falling into the clutches of the prison industrial complex, must become important across the board.

We must seek out those organizations which have similar objectives, where a coalition is possible. One such organization is "The Justice Lobby" out of Pittsburgh, PA, which is seeking to reform the prison system in this nation. I agree with their philosophy, that in order to change the prison system, you must organize the people who are most affected. The people who are impacted by crime, by drugs, by death, are the inmates, the ex-offenders, and their families and concerned community residents, and they can bring about a change when they stand together and organize.

History does not provide reliable data suggesting the right way to stop violence. Thus, to use a greater level of violence, in order to curb the present epidemic of killings across black America, will only cause more violence. The problems that cause the violence in the first place will be left unresolved. This will only cause the violence to occur, and reoccur, placing before the black American living within the walls of the inner city, an early death, or certain incarceration.

The black American is held up before the eyes of the world as a violence prone individual, with few, if any, redeeming values. We must stop worrying about the world, and focus on what is required to bring change into our lives. Education is the key to reclaiming control over our lives and communities, which started going downhill with the coming of one way integration. A people that truly know who they are, are less likely to wish genocide upon themselves, or their people.

DISAVOWING THE ADDICTION TO VIOLENCE...

    When the slaves first came upon this native land, they were not greeted with violence. Yet, they came in the name of violence, and we have known violence from that period, to the present.

    To the black American caught up in the world of the ex-offender, and seeking positive change, The National Association of Brothers and Sisters In & Out (NABSIO), is the organization for you. It is wise to keep in mind the fact, "Our Creator didn't bring us into the reality of life, to be violent towards each other."

Chapter 7

HOW EDUCATION, THE AFROCENTRIC WAY, WORKS

Finding out that functional illiteracy and historical ignorance are so widespread throughout America's prison industrial complex, so angered me I felt compelled to act. How I would act was not clear at the moment the thought entered my mind. But act I would. It was some weeks later that my willingness to do something started taking shape.

What I really needed was information—information that only the inmates themselves could provide. At the time my knowledge of prison life was zero. Never having been behind the walls of my first prison, all I had was a burning anger in the pit of my stomach, that said to me, "You can make a difference if you try," and try I did.

First, I went after the information needed to provide a starting point, writing letters to anyone at the California State Prison, at Corcoran, California, through a contact who had at one time been incarcerated at that facility. The information gave me a clear view, in my mind just how and where was the best place to start.

Other blessings started coming into my life, that helped shape my thinking. Brother Nathaniel Perkins-Ali came forward to join this vision to make a difference in the lives of any African-American inmate seeking a positive change in their lives.

Behind prison walls are some of black America's best brain power. It was to this area I directed my letters, by requesting that those I was in contact with, help to get my address in the hands of the inmates who they felt were Afrocentric in their thinking. Not long after making that request, a letter came from William H. Jackson, an inmate with a keen mind, that was eager to join our efforts to create a program that could make a difference in fighting against functional and historical ignorance.

Not only was inmate Jackson willing to join our ranks, he was the one that wrote NABSIO's first Afrocentric curriculum—a curriculum that makes use of textbooks that are written by African/African-American authors.

After inmate Jackson accepted the position of Director of Education for the National Association of Brothers and Sisters In & Out, our program, centering around Afrocentric education sent out the word—NABSIO was signing up inmate students.

One of the first facilities to respond to our call for students, was the California prison in Lancaster, California. There were some thirteen inmates in the first group to sign up. The next step was to get the textbooks in the hands of this group. After purchasing the textbooks from the Eso Won book store, and providing the address where they were to be shipped, our program was activated.

This was a first, working from afar with men who were locked down for being involved in some form of crime, that caused them to be taking this program from behind prison walls. Finding out their mindset, would not be an easy task. What we hoped would happen was, each inmate would establish a close relationship, through the mail, with our NABSIO main office. We wanted to waste no time in building a strong bond with these, our first inmate students, that could carry over to our next group.

It didn't take long to find out our vision wasn't about to become a success, without committed key individuals that had the ability to direct the study from within. And who had a burning passion for NABSIO's mission.

The next obstacle we had to overcome, was selecting new textbooks because our current textbooks were at a level slightly above our first group. So we had to start from the beginning, by writing new study guides and exams for each text. Thus, the way forward was both slow and very informative. This obstacle challenged our own commitment to our vision. Letters were coming in from throughout the California prison industrial complex. Thus, the idea to write a battery of pre-enrollment exams worked to our advantage, because this bought us the necessary time to write our new study guides and end of text exams—which was no small task.

Our anchor text was written by Dr. Jawanza Kunjufu, under the title, "Lessons From History: A Celebration In Blackness." This is a wonderful text for introducing the study of our history, in a well-organized manner. And this text helped us to understand, this was not going to be easy teaching our history from afar, which only inspired our desire to press forward with as much fervor as possible.

Even when we were making a strong effort to become known and trusted behind prison walls, our mail volume continued to increase from Corcoran, and Lancaster State Prisons. Inmates who were outside our initial program, wanted very aggressively to study the history of the black man.

As fast as I would learn of one problem or another, I would get the information into the hands of Education Director Jackson, at Corcoran State Prison. He never failed to give his mind over to solving our problems, one after another. In the process, my knowledge of operating a correspondence school grew into a mindset, which confirmed what I already knew: correspondence education is a way of dealing with teaching black history, that can and will reach thousands of inmates throughout America's prisons.

History is just the first step in this vision. Social responsibility is the next step in this ever-evolving process, for getting inside the minds of inmates seeking an avenue back on to the main road. Spirituality is the entity so vital in the lives of all African-Americans, that seeks positive change in the American nightmare known as the prison industrial complex.

Prior to NABSIO, there were no Afrocentric education programs in existence, to our knowledge. We are our own model. We learn by doing, sink or swim, as we move deeper, and deeper into uncharted waters.

We searched throughout the California prison system, seeking allies that could become NABSIO's strong arms behind prison walls, to help build a strong program. We worked to convince our people in prison, that all is not lost, if we would but turn to education in order to have better lives in the future.

This future we cannot depend on others to secure for our benefit.

HOW EDUCATION THE AFROCENTRIC WAY WORKS

It is not written anywhere, that we cannot work together in order to strengthen our own futures. NABSIO is building towards that future with every fiber of its willpower.

Within the near future, we look forward to having one of our leading black universities, offer a Bachelor of Arts degree in Afrocentricity. The NABSIO Education Plan is not a begging plan, that will not work if there are no monies coming in from the federal government. This plan stands squarely on the shoulders of those blacks that want their minds free of depending on others, for what they themselves can accomplish.

Getting involved with the NABSIO vision for Afrocentric education only requires a letter, requesting a relationship with the most revolutionary educational programs to hit the black community since the publication of Dr. Carter G. Woodson's, "The Miseducation of the Negro."

Bold? Yes! Too bold? No! No program is forthcoming from outside the black community, that will rescue the imprisoned minds of black people. To stand by and wait for the descendants of slave owners to provide factual education about black people, is insane! So NABSIO, and its allies, both in and out of prison, developed the following plan:

Objectives:

> To encourage and promote academic and vocational training available within correctional institutions; To encourage each inmate/student to seek a personal relationship with our Creator; and to encourage each potential inmate/student interested in becoming a par-

FROM MISEDUCATION TO INCARCERATION

ticipant within the NABSIO Leisure Time Study Group, to get a sponsor from among the facility staff. Then submit a written request to the facility manager for class space. Once approval is granted, NABSIO, as the primary outside sponsor, will issue one textbook per student, to be used to teach African/African-American history, social responsibility, and spirituality (religion and African Philosophy).

PROGRAM REQUIREMENTS:

1.) All inmates/students, prior to acceptance into the NABSIO Leisure Time Study Group, should be currently enrolled in, or on a waiting list for, academic or vocational training when available. However, when such training is not available, this will not in anyway prevent the inmate from being eligible to enroll in NABSIO's Group Studies Ministry, by organizing with other interested inmates in a leisure time activity class, for Afrocentric growth.
2.) All inmates/students should do their best to remain disciplinary free while enrolled in this ministry.
3.) All written assignments will be controlled by the inmate group teacher, as will the length of time required to complete each text.

COURSE DESCRIPTION:

This is not an easy program, nor was it designed to be. The emphasis is on more than the subject matter, it is

HOW EDUCATION THE AFROCENTRIC WAY WORKS

also on perfecting writing skills, not so much writing skills in the mechanical sense, but in putting your thoughts down on paper. This course will challenge you to not only examine the course material, but to also interpret and explain the material in your own words. This ministry further challenges you to teach this knowledge to others around you.

TEACHING METHOD:

Textbooks will be issued in the order requested by the class leader. Once all lessons for each assigned text, along with the completed assignments are turned in and receive a minimum passing grade of 70%, the student will then be issued a 100 question multiple choice test on the same text. This 100 question test is a closed book test. After the full class has satisfactorily completed this test, and returned it to NABSIO's main office for grading, the class will then be issued the next text requested by the class leader.

Chapter 8

THE LOSS OF A DAUGHTER

February 27, 1999, high noon on Central and Broxton Avenues, Riverside, California, on the site where Tyisha Miller, who had only enjoyed 19 years of the life God had blessed her with, was killed by four out-of-control police from the Riverside Police Department.

This was two months ago, still there are questions the police refuse to answer, questions the Riverside DA refuses to answer, questions the Mayor of Riverside refuses to answer. To say they don't have the answers the African-American community is asking, is to insult the intelligence of those doing the asking. The Miller-Butler families, Tyisha's family, have a right to know.

FROM MISEDUCATION TO INCARCERATION

On this day, I stood on the spot where Tyisha died, from the bullets that angrily pierced her young body as if she was some rabid animal, and not a young female in need of help. I stood there, looking around at the sea of faces, that were there, perhaps as I was, hoping to find some answers to this madness, that truly poses a danger to America, from coast to coast. The questions not yet answered are hard questions, and they require hard answers, that the power structure seems unwilling to provide, for whatever reason.

Just three miles from this location, I too have a part of my family, with two granddaughters that are Tyisha's peers. They travel this same route that should have been safe for Tyisha. A well lighted service station, open 24 hours a day, should prove safe for anyone— "anyone that is not black like Sister Tyisha." If this is the wrong answer, then those that feel they have the right answers, should step forward, and let the community hear what they have to offer.

Not far from Riverside, I have two other granddaughters that drive cars, and could, at any given moment, develop car trouble, or like Tyisha become ill and need help. I fear for their safety, and must bring into operation a 911 family plan that will protect my family from a system that continues to step back from this area of responsibility. It's a sad day in America when you call 911, and the police come with death, not help. This is reality, that a black man must protect his family by any means necessary.

We must say to the system, and mean it unto death, "We have no more Tyisha Millers that you can murder and then walk away." We are a people that have a God that is all powerful, and we should not weaken this power by being full of fear; this is killing our children.

The hunting season must be declared ended, by no less than the President of these United States. All powers of authority must want the same safety for our Tyishas, as they want for their Janes.

THE LOSS OF A DAUGHTER

Yes, there are those within the African-American community that know the answers to the questions those in positions of local power refuse to answer. We know you go behind closed doors, to make your decisions among yourselves. Our child Tyisha was taken ill while "black," needed help while "black," did not receive help—only murder. Now it is important that her tragic death must help to save the other Tyishas that will continue to "drive while black," thinking they are safe if they are in need of assistance, in the middle of the night, on America's streets that are becoming more and more dangerous at the movement of this nation's time clock of racism and hatred.

There were a few outstanding leaders and celebrities present on this occasion. The Reverend Jesse Jackson was there, leading a sizable number of local clergy, blacks and whites. Danny Bakewell, Sr., of the Los Angeles-based Brotherhood Crusade, and Dr. Sandra Moore of the Congress of Racial Equality, under the directorship of State Chairman Celes King III, of Los Angeles were there.

The person that did it for me, on this spiritual occasion, was highly popular "Baby Face" and his lovely wife. I think what really touched me, was the fact he came to open his heart to the Miller-Butler Family, in honor of the loss of their child.

It is not the beautiful lyrics of a song that is the measure of a man or woman. If this was true, the "Baby Faces," the "Stevie Wonders," and the "Harry Belafontes" would be heads and shoulders above many of their contemporaries.

It is the heart and spirit of these individuals that march to the collective heartbeat of their people. Whenever I hear their music being played, I not only enjoy their music, but am made to feel that I am a better person, due to the artistry I sense in it.

After the gathering had grown to over several hundred, we were formed into a mass demonstration, and marched to downtown Riverside. Here more speakers took the stand and lambasted the police department for holding back on what the majority felt was the real evidence in this case. No matter how this story was told, it was clear Tyisha Miller should not have lost her life the way she did, only to have leadership in Riverside remain silent, in hopes of keeping the lid on the money they knew the city would have to give up for the negligent loss of a child. This information only infuriated the demonstrators all the more.

This pattern would be followed for more than a year on a weekly basis. Cars and buses came down from Los Angeles, loaded with many activists that felt this kind of racism is often never corrected. The government waits for the family to sue, then finds a price that everyone can live with, pays the money, then moves on, hoping some trigger-happy cop doesn't kill other innocent victims, while the community of African-Americans is still inflamed.

However, there are too many racist cops throughout the state of California for someone among them to refrain from killing another innocent person.

I continued making the trip down to Riverside, week after week, to add my presence to the demonstration. I was always dressed in my Afrocentric attire, with rich African colors that really stand out, when the T.V. camera catches me in its lens. Standing some three inches over six feet, it would be hard to miss me, seeing as how very few African-Americans are willing to dress in Afrocentric fashions. With me, this is who I am. So what better way is there for me to tell you who I am by the way I dress?

Each time I would meet with the inmates at the California Institute for Women in Corona, California, they would tell me they saw me at the demonstration in Riverside, on the evening news. They

THE LOSS OF A DAUGHTER

always seemed to feel a part of what I was doing, in seeking justice for Tyisha Miller.

My next big event in Riverside came on the day a large number of demonstrators was arrested for civil disobedience, for blocking the main entrance to the Riverside Police Department. What was so special about this arrest, is the fact some of the biggest names in civil protest were among those of us being arrested. Perhaps the biggest name was none other than Dick Gregory, who had gone to jail many times with Dr. Martin Luther King, Jr., in many places throughout the southern part of the country, only to come full circle in sunny Riverside, California and end up going to jail with Martin Luther King III, the eldest son of the late Dr. Martin Luther King, Jr. Also arrested was Kim Fields, star of the popular sitcom "Living Single." She was not playing a part on this day, which was easy to see from her display of temper as she expressed herself to the arresting officers. At first I didn't know who the cute little sister was, that was giving the police a good piece of her mind. She must be all of five feet tall, and she was talking to an officer that stands well over six feet. That didn't seem to bother her at all, she was determined to have her say, and have her say she did.

The next time I ran into her was in Los Angeles, at another rally on behalf of another African-American female, shot down by yet another trigger-happy police officer. I walked over to her to introduce myself, and to ask if I could give her a big brotherly hug of appreciation, for being the human being that she is. She walked into my arms just like any of my four daughters, or my twelve granddaughters. These are the kind of rewards you get as an activist, when you stand for what is right and just.

Being jailed with Dr. Sandra Moore of Los Angeles made it possible for me to hold my head a little higher, each time I stepped

FROM MISEDUCATION TO INCARCERATION

inside the women's prison on my weekly visits with the inmates at CIW Corona.

To many black people being arrested is a disgrace; whereas with me it is a disgrace to do nothing when the police can kill a young girl, and many of our people stand around as if this behavior is all right. If there is a disgrace in going to jail for standing up for what's right, there truly must be shame connected to being a coward.

I think those that were arrested that day, in the city where my six children were born, during my service to this nation in the US Air Force, are all heroes, in my way of seeing the world.

I will always feel the Miller Family's pain. Just as I will always feel America's pain. Because I realize she will never be as great, or as beautiful as she could be, if she can never find the way to become a just nation. So far, the great numbers of New Africans behind bars say she still has a long way to go. When the most powerful nation on this planet continues to send its less fortunate citizens to prison for the rest of their lives, in response to petty crimes, we can see how far she has to go, to be truly a great country. The functional illiteracy rate is far below the numbers released by the Little Hoover Commission. Los Angeles Times, Friday, November 14, 2003 reported, "Percentage of parolees who are functionally illiterate: 50%." All of this is part of America's pain, just as is the deaths of her daughters at the hands of killer cops out of control!

When killer cops start going to jail for their crimes, and the Tyisha Millers can live out their lives in safety, America will be well on her way to becoming great.

Chapter 9

SHAKA'S LAST VOTE

In Washington D.C., October 16, the city where some million plus of my brothers stood with me in the most awe-inspiring event of my life, now known as "The Million Man March," my life changed forever.

Now, August 17, 2002, I'm standing on the same grounds where some of the men stood that October 16, 1995. Only this time things are not the same. Where I stood before for the first gathering in October 1995, has been closed to the public since the 911 attack on America.

However, this rally that I had returned to in Washington, D.C. to

FROM MISEDUCATION TO INCARCERATION

attend, was held in sight of the Capital where I stood for the Million Man March, still some distance away from this event. This was a rally to tell the power brokers of America of the seriousness of the black American's claim for REPARATION.

There are so many reasons why all blacks should look to America to settle this debt. There are many ways this debt could be paid. For me, I would like to see the opportunity for real education to take place throughout black America from kindergarten to the graduate degree.

Through **REPARATION** the nation would be in a position to correct many ills, caused by a criminal system that tries to keep those seeking to be compensated for previous wrongs, in deprivation, and absolute fear of the very government that should offer its protection.

America has always stood for the power of the vote. One man or woman, one vote. These are the thoughts that ran around in my mind as I stood among the large crowd present to add their voices to that of others, for the black man's **REPARATION** some two hundred years overdue.

The power brokers of this nation control the vote of the majority by playing on their fears, using the influence of the major media outlets, in order to go into each home with a T.V. or radio, to push code words with racist and white supremist undertones, for the purpose of getting the vote to go in the direction they desire.

When you are a powerless people, there is very little you can do to prevent this behavior. One of the sure ways of controlling the vote through fear, is to send out the message you will be hard on crime if elected.

To have a high profile African-American in the public's eye at the time of an upcoming election, is votes in the ballot box, if you can keep him (the black criminal), in his place. Such was the case during the last national election.

Gary Graham, a death row inmate in the state of Texas, was

fighting for his life, for a crime it is obvious he was not guilty of. However, his vote, in the form of his death, would go far in turning out the vote for the party in power. After all, wasn't it a white man this black criminal killed? What does it matter that he was not given a fair trial? His vote was needed at this point, in the voting booth known to those on death row as the death chamber.

I don't make accusations I cannot provide sound evidence for. For example, there was no DNA evidence against Gary Graham, no gunpowder on his hands, showing he had just fired a gun. Even the gun he had in his possession was not the murder weapon. Only a single eye witness testified seeing Gary, 40 to 60 feet away, at night, for a few seconds, when there were at a very minimum, two other witnesses that swore the state was holding the wrong man. They were never called to give their testimony. You would have to question why this oversight—if it was an oversight.

By this time, on Gary's timeline to death, he had gone through a metamorphosis. Gary Graham was his slave name going in, and he was Shaka Sankofa, a strong Afrocentric warrior, coming out.

Shaka was a troubled youth that earned a long rap sheet, which was used to put him in an unmarked grave in Houston, Texas. Like so many other African-American youth, Shaka lived a confused life, one that caused him to be murdered in the end.

He would have been standing among his brothers at the Million Man March, if not for his incarceration for a crime he did not commit. His murder only stilled his body, and gave strength to his spirit that dwells within my soul. I humbly beseech any African-American that reads these words, to stop and ask yourself just what does this land called America mean to you.

Let me tell you what it means to this black man. It is a land where many of my relatives died at the hands of evil individuals. A beautiful land, a land that our Native American brothers/sisters enjoyed

FROM MISEDUCATION TO INCARCERATION

many, many years before the European and African man came, bringing with them the ability to change something beautiful into something that rides a pale horse—death.

Thanks to the spirit of the "Million Man March" I can still appreciate the basic good in the majority of Americans, in spite of the evil that always seeks to influence the good. This is where my family live. My children, my grandchildren, my great grandchildren, all make their homes in this land. How could I not love this land, and be willing to give my life to defend it, from any enemy within or without? Especially from within.

Two very beautiful extended families spread all over this land give me another reason to love America. It also provides me with the spiritual strength to see the wrong in killing an innocent man in order to win an election. This is the land I love, the land that will murder an innocent man, and feel no guilt.

An independent film producer made a thirteen-minute film showing why Shaka Sankofa, an innocent man, was killed. This film is kept at the NABSIO main office in Los Angeles, where it can be viewed upon request. Then you can make up your own mind about the killing of Shaka Sankofa.

The state of Texas did not let all of the evidence on behalf of Shaka be presented in court. This evidence tells us, his alleged victim died with $6,000 on his person. But the state convicted him of robbery and murder.

This is the part of Shaka's story that speaks to my spirit. After the state had used his death to cast a vote for being hard on crime, nothing was worked out to see that his remains were given a proper burial. Perhaps, you wonder why should I expect the state to give him a proper burial. I don't.

Since the information was given to me by Ricky Jason, of Beaumount, Texas, during my last visit while in the South, I have been involved in keeping Shaka's spirit alive, in my love and respect for what's important to me as an African-American, that wants all people to be treated fairly, throughout this nation. Not only was Shaka not treated fairly, in no stretch of the imagination can it be shown that Shaka received justice from those who held the power to take his life unjustly.

Shaka's remains are waiting in the ground with no proper grave marker in the city of Houston, Texas. Houston is the largest city in Texas, with a population of well over a million residents. Right in the midst of this million plus residents, there must be a memorial at Shaka's gravesite, to remind us of the duty placed on all people of just hearts and fair minds, by the Creator of all mankind.

As long as the death penalty remains the law of the land in most states, there are evil individuals who will continue to use this law for evil, and not just purposes.

It was wrong to kill Shaka for a crime he was not guilty of. Just as it's wrong to sit back and let these killings continue, without doing all in our power to end this uncivilized behavior, which weakens our position as leaders of the free world. It places our government on the same level as other murderers.

My commitment to the spirit of Shaka Sankofa is to continue to seek an end to the death penalty, throughout the States. This book shall serve as a means to raise funds to erect a memorial at the gravesite of Shaka.

It is important to work on helping troubled youth, who think crime is the only way for them to survive. It was Shaka's early teen problems that ultimately caused his downfall. Helping troubled youth heading into a life of crime, by showing them another direction, is another way to tell Shaka how much we regret as a people not being there for him, in his greatest hour of need.

Chapter 10

UNIVERSITY OF THE MIND

If I know nothing else, I know if you believe in something hard enough and are willing to work, day after day to make it happen, it can happen. Another thing I have become aware of over the years of my life, is there are sayings that have been around for years that we take for granted, that we think are truisms based on their longevity alone, like the saying that old men see visions, and young men dream dreams.

I am neither young nor old. For the past seventy-six years I have been living among my people, and on occasions I have lived among others not of my ethnicity, sometimes for long periods at a time, always feeling on the cutting edge of insecurity. Not really being wanted, in the church, in the clubs, or just any social gathering. There was always a knot in the pit of my stomach, telling me something wasn't right. It would be wonderful if I could pinpoint the day when the knot was no longer there. It's really not critical to the issue at hand. What I can tell you is this, I was still in the military on duty in West Germany when the knot disappeared.

What did it for me was a story that was published in the "Stars and Stripes" newspaper, printed overseas for the American reading public, about a shoot-out between a New Orleans Panther Chapter, and the police in that area. There was a photo that appeared with the story that presented a view of a canvas bucket, filled with spent shotgun shells. After reading the story and viewing the photo very closely, the African conscience became stronger in my mind. I could clearly see that story was not completely true, and that the photo could have been, and no doubt was, a poorly rigged job by the police. A driving force was created within my spirit that cannot stand idly by and see what white supremacy is doing under the guise of miseducation and illiteracy, and do nothing.

The dreams that I am having are more nightmares than pleasant dreams. Nightmares because I no longer hear the voice of that one of ones, the late Dr. Martin Luther King, Jr., weaving me a spell about dreams. Thus, the nightmares come each time an African child dies in the streets where many nightmares are made for too many African mothers, who cry out for their men to put a stop to this madness, all across this nation.

My visions no longer have the voice of that gallant warrior of the conscience of the black man, Malcolm X, to point our attack against the institutions of white supremacy. Although my dreams may leave a lot to be desired, my visions are working overtime, if not all the time.

UNIVERSITY OF THE MIND

Along the way I have met and known many black men. Some I still try to contact from time to time. Others I just let them drift out of my mind. But I keep close those that are caught up in the visions that are as much a part of my spirit, as my understanding of who I am in relationship to my Creator.

There are only two New African brothers, and one definition of a vision, found in the American Heritage College Dictionary. I have already told you about one of these two men, caught up in my dreams, my visions and indeed my world—Nathaniel Perkins. You will come to know more about this African, and I hope and pray you will also come to love him, because he is a son, he is a brother, he is a warrior for the people to me, and he is all New African to me.

My life was given great meaning because I became truly pissed with a system that will lock a man/woman down, in many cases for little or no legal reason, and seek to keep them in a high state of horrific illiteracy and unadulterated ignorance.

The definition of a vision is "Unusual competence in discernment or perception; intelligent foresight." The second brother was seated at the table in my mind, where the vision came to me that told me to look to ancient Egypt for the answer to this vision. Thus, was born the concept of the University of the Mind.

Did my spiritual protector have me visit ancient Egypt in my mind, in order to show me something about that period before there was anything there? I think so. When there was only sand for miles around, the ancient people had no vast array of equipment to accomplish what the world now know they accomplished. When they first came to that location, Egypt was only in their minds, and the world was blessed to untold heights. This was as clear in my mind as if I was there in person. My first impression was that I must find others whose spirits are telling them these same truths.

Remember this name, Abdul Olugbala Shakur. He is now seated

at the table, flowing his scholarship into my spirit, in what seems to be a never ending source of pure New African love for our people. Why have our two spirits not crossed before I made my spiritual trip to ancient Egypt? He, like myself, has been seeking a conduit for his scholarship to flow out to his people for a lengthy period of time.

For the reader that may be experiencing some difficulty in going with me as we talk about a university in our minds, let our brother Ray Charles help you to understand. Buy his recording of "America the Beautiful", and sit down and listen to this recording with no one else around. Tell your mind to show you what Brother Ray Charles sees with his mind when he is singing this song.

He is not using his eyes, because as we know, the eyes can often blind us to the truth. This genius in the recording business is using his mind to see, and his voice to tell us what his mind saw.

Brother Abdul Olugbala Shakur is letting his scholarship flow out into the turbulent waters of white supremacy and black apathy inviting any brother/sister living out their lives behind the walls of this nation's present day slave system, to come forward and present your scholarship to the newly formed "Council of Scholars." And be prepared to accomplish literary feats that even you may not be aware are possible.

My passion is to move against the crippling affliction affecting New African people in America, known as functional and cultural illiteracy, both inside prisons and inside the public school system across this land. On this point I have bonded with my spiritual son, Abdul Olugbala Shakur, to the degree I hurry to push myself in visions, into his dreams, into his nightmares, to the extent that he will know I am there with him in his cell, each night, when his mind is troubled.

The prison industrial slave complex now houses one continuous

UNIVERSITY OF THE MIND

flow of New African University campuses under the name of the George Jackson University. This was all born from the founder's vision that came into my mind from Abdul Olugbala Shakur.

There are those of us that cannot, and will not, let white supremacy get away with bringing slavery back, by sending many of the best brains our people have produced to waste away in cells made of concrete and steel.

Some of us are aware of the harm white so-called scholars attempt to accomplish with their racist findings, about black people. I need to give you a brief glimpse into the scholastic strength of Abdul Olugbala Shakur, in dealing with white supremacy:

If White America can find logic in the <u>Bell Curve</u> theory, then they should have no problem with its opposite, which I now propose and shall call the <u>Curve Bell</u> theory. In this society and our country, sexual assault, child molestation, and the abduction of children are becoming an epidemic, and according to all statistics the White male is the primary perpetrator of these heinous crimes against the children. How do we protect our children, the most vulnerable of our society, from crimes of this nature? At The Institute for Advanced Reverse Discrimination, the social scientists, Shaka Zulu and Queen Nzinga, are proposing that federal funding be allocated towards research to discover the gene, which causes the white male between the ages of 30 to 50 to inflict such perverted sickness on children. Hopefully, we can identify, and neutralize this gene by way of medication or by its surgical removal. And while we're at it, why not remove the gene that causes the White man to feel superior to the black man? (You know this gene that has caused millions of deaths.) When our research is complete, the White male will be reduced to a medicated vegetable, but at least he'll be cured of all his genetic illnesses. World peace could then be accomplished without the white man's corrupted involvement. These white males shouldn't complain about being vegetables; it's better than slavery or being forced to live in impoverished colonial ghettos. At least, in this reversed experiment, we weren't so harsh as to impose a discovery of Europe by the black man! The point I am making is that there's no logic or reasoning to Bell Curve. If you can find moral reasoning in Bell Curve, you should have no problem in finding it in Curve Bell.

This is only a thumbnail sketch of Abdul Olugbala Shakur's analysis of the <u>Bell Curve</u>. You can find more in his complete study and analysis of this subject in his writings found in "Ghetto Criminology: A Brief Analysis Of America Criminalizing A Race."

I am firmly convinced the answer to the crime problem facing black America will be found behind prison walls, among these New African thinkers sitting at the table of the George Jackson University. These are the ones whose minds have dissected the field of criminology, in ways that would amaze some criminologists. To even attempt to amaze anyone in the white world, is not where these scholars are headed with their scholarship. Their direction is centered in finding the keys needed to unlock doors, long closed to Africans seeking truths concerning black life in this nation.

Our families with relatives in prison will have to become more proactive, in dealing with their male children, if they hope to keep them out of the clutches of the system that seeks to incarcerate them for life at an early age. Our scholarship will reach out to these families in such a way, it will be made clear what actions to take in order to receive help.

There will be those that will oppose this very revolutionary approach to fighting our way out of this white supremacist inferno.

UNIVERSITY OF THE MIND

They will not all be white. Always, in the midst of any movement that seeks to lift the black man/woman up from their situation of slavery, standing among the community are the blacks that are always willing to live their existence locked in a state of mental slavery just so long as white people are not pissed off. This is an attitude the New African thinkers will have to analyze at some point in the future.

We must use our minds in ways that can free our people from behaving as slaves. There are millions who have been negatively affecting our people through the criminal system, giving the world the idea that the descendents of the slave in this nation are evil, and the high rate of crime is caused by New African people. Using our minds as a weapon is an important process in understanding why our people are given such long and hard sentences, why there are more blacks in prison than there are any other people. You don't have to have a college degree to use your mind. All New African people have the genes that were in our ancient people who gave the world its first known civilizations. Any student of the George Jackson University will always be challenged to become a warrior for New African people, in their never ending struggle to receive protection from that all elusive entity called justice, and not just-us.

You are not required to pay a tuition fee for enrollment in the University of the Mind. However, you should purge your mind of all fear of white supremacy. That is important in becoming a freedom fighter for justice. Feeding the mind spirit food, can be one way of purging it of fear. Knowing the true history of New African people is the strongest mind food you will ever need, to accomplish the purging exercise. Once you start on this road there can be no turning back. You must continue forward until you reach the free sands of ancient Egypt in your mind's eye.

You are always invited to enroll at the University of the Mind campus, the tuition is free, the hours are long, the reward is great. The degree you will earn is entitled, "Know Thyself."

Chapter 11

FUNCTIONAL ILLITERACY IS A KILLER

In the past twelve years we have talked about the plague of functional illiteracy, wanting to do something to bring an end to this affliction among black inmates throughout the prison industrial complex, with nothing more than talk to show for this desire. We have wanted to formalize a plan from day one of our organization's existence, to start down the long road to lift this damaging albatross from around the neck of black inmates.

It doesn't take an Imhotep to deduce that neither the State of California, nor the Federal government, is likely to care about this affliction, because it is not financially profitable. We are also aware it doesn't take a great genius to understand the inability of our churches and social organizations to address this issue, for reasons known only to them and our Creator. With the problem growing larger with each day the criminal justice system is on the job, and large numbers of functionally illiterate New Africans continue to fall prey to America's white supremacist behavior towards black people.

The answer to any given problem is already locked away in our minds, if we would only look there for answers that we sometimes are reluctant to find. I now realize the help needed to start down this road leading to a war against functional illiteracy is already behind bars, in the minds of some of the best brains black America has produced.

There is no black American living that knows any better than I do, that inside of the minds of many black inmates can be found the solution to this problem. Realizing no help is likely to come from any other source, I have already sent my ideas into the minds of some of the best thinkers among black Americans, to raise up a "Council of Scholars" willing to bond with thinkers on this side of the prison walls, by creating a "University of the Mind."

This vision, like the vision to create the National Association of Brothers and Sisters In & Out (NABSIO), is necessary to expose the wall of silence involving the miseducation of the black inmate. We must take this idea from within our minds, and devise a plan of action like the plans to build the first civilization in the minds of our ancestors.

Before our ancestors could give to the world the first civilization, they had only their minds to work with, just as we have our minds to work with. Once our "Council of Scholars" is in place, an action plan can be devised to move forward against this affliction we call functional illiteracy, making it possible to reach, and teach many brothers

FUNCTIONAL ILLITERACY IS A KILLER

and sisters behind prison walls, that truly need our strength and wisdom.

Thus, the door of need stands wide open, for any brother or sister that wants to join this university, join the minds of those on the front line fighting this war on the battlefield of educational denial.

When the African was no longer needed as a cheap labor source in America, we were in deep trouble. Funds to educate black children were not flowing into the coffers of school boards, in the inner cities where the majority of black children are being miseducated. These funds now had another purpose, that would still touch the lives of these same miseducated inner city youth. Schools of a different hue—the prison industrial complex.

No section of the country offer a better example of how this madness works, than right here in the State of California. First, in the past two decades, California went on a prison-building frenzy that could not be equaled by any other state, although some gave it their best shot.

Along with this prison building frenzy, there were laws passed to insure these prisons would always be filled to capacity. How else can the justice be explained in a law that will see you given three life sentences, plus twenty years, for conspiracy to sell five kilograms of cocaine? And, the cocaine was never placed before the court as evidence, just the word of a racist drug agent that was willing to lie, in order to make himself look good in the eyes of his equally racist superiors in the Drug Enforcement Administration.

California has the worst laws on the books being used to keep prison beds filled with sleepers, for many years, into the future of this state. The web woven around the politics of this state, involving prisons, would make even a spider proud. The three strikes law, that was presented to the voting public as the means of keeping danger-

FROM MISEDUCATION TO INCARCERATION

ous criminals locked up for life, was all a big lie. For it has been proven this is just a tool in the hands of lying politicians, corrupt justice department officials, crooked police, and power-hungry prosecuting attorneys. From one end of America to the other end, they are all sleeping in the same bed of slimy greed.

Any prison that is warehousing large numbers of black inmates is a potential university, with brothers and sisters waiting for help, any help that is positive in nature, and Afrocentric principled, reaching out a helping hand to any African-American inmate that wishes to change the directions of his/her life cycle, and move away from a mindset of crime.

Fighting cultural ignorance, or functional illiteracy, is no cakewalk. For those that choose this way of life, there are no days you should not be prepared to understand just what the true situation is for black families, when they have relatives behind the walls of a prison. Then we can truly understand just how really tragic the lives of a large percentage of black Americans are. Many inmates' family members themselves are functional illiterates, due in part to being in a country that really has no true love for black people. Our very existence is a constant reminder of how we have been treated by the whites of this country. The world looks at America and sees blacks and whites always at odds. Why? No persons, be they black or white, if they are fair-minded, can say this nation has ever opened its heart to the black man, in feelings of true love. Thus, why should we continue to expect anything but miseducation of our people by this system?

Functional illiteracy is not a phenomenon that was born behind prison walls, nor is cultural ignorance. Both of these killers of black people, are as American as apple pie. If we were to track any given black inmate who is functionally illiterate, on a time line from the ghetto to prison, we could possibly learn a few facts—ones that could

FUNCTIONAL ILLITERACY IS A KILLER

help in reducing future levels of functional illiteracy behind prison bars.

In evolving a plan that will be useful to those behind bars, who will become the teachers of those in need, we must make sure our "Council of Scholars" receives the best support possible, in order for them to produce the best results possible. There must always be a level of equal dialogue between the university staff and the CDC, when proper recognition is extended to the Council of Scholars.

The Center for Disease Control and Prevention released information about the high rate of HIV among black women, but no explanation as to why this behavior is so prevalent among blacks. Education is not even mentioned as a possible causal factor. Not the education that tells you the best way to be safe is not to have sex. The true education of any individual should be the education that helps the individual to develop a healthy value system.

If we truly care about our people that need help, talk to your minister about taking the lock off the church door on Saturday. Then get the parents with their children to come forth to create a school that can teach our people about life, not lies. We are a hurting, and a badly damaged people. We fear commitment to education. When we participated in slavery against our will, we were willing to die for education. Just to read and write cost the lives of many slaves. Today, many of our people think all black people are free. Thus, they feel each one should be personally motivated to get an education, should have the moral decency to not have intercourse, without using protection. That's right, should have!

For those of you that took your little penis out of your pants at an early age, as I did, for the purpose of getting between some girl's legs, didn't anyone tell you this is not a game between boys and girls? There was no conscious effort to harm any girl, just the joy of using

FROM MISEDUCATION TO INCARCERATION

sexual powers before the brain was equipped with the right data to do so wisely. Are the children to be found guilty, who haven't received the correct training to live in a world where educated people create diseases to kill uneducated people? And there are those in the black community that know this to be true, and still stand on the sidelines to watch the game of life pass by hoping that functional and cultural illiteracy will soon move off stage, putting HIV and AIDS behind them. Not so!

We should not be so trusting as to think someone in our State Capitals, or Federal Government will, out of the goodness of their hearts, care less than pig shit about how many black people are functional illiterates, have HIV, AIDS, or just bad health period.

That's not the worst part. The worst part is how little we care about these conditions, holding our people in a state of incarceration is just as mentally damaging to black people as the Segregated Housing Unit, at the slave-breaking prison known as Pelican Bay State Prison, in the State of California.

In speaking to black America, I say, "There always comes a time where one has to put up, or shut up." Our time is now as war clouds are already gathering over our people. Trust me, I know. For I am part of a people who have been in a continuous struggle for over four hundred years. Check your history, don't let historical illiteracy keep you in the dark.

Chapter **12**

THE MIRRORS IN MY SOUL

Who is it that said, "A country is never greater than its treatment of those it holds in its prisons?" Each time I receive news of some cruel and inhumane act, within the walls of some prisons within this state, I am sickened to the pits of my very being. Treatment that would let a wad of newspaper be given to a female prisoner, to be used for excessive bleeding with her menstrual cycle; assigning an inmate to a cell where there is a predator rapist, waiting for the next victim to be placed in its web of control. These are but two of the more extreme humiliating acts that have come to my knowledge, of a man and a

FROM MISEDUCATION TO INCARCERATION

woman, that have been wronged right here in the State of California's prison systems.

What does this tell us about ourselves, when we let those that commit these acts against us, get off without being severely punished for their evil deeds? These evil deeds escaped punishment, because of some justice officials' and politicians' fear of appearing to be weak on criminals, in order to win and protect their office and racist careers. What does it say about our churches that know these acts are being committed, and remain silent? If I know these acts are being committed, they, too, have access to the same information. The only difference is I refuse to be silent.

Looking back on the past ten years, my life has been an exercise in stimulating motivational Afrocentric growth, which has, in turn, enhanced my spiritual well-being that I feel in my existence. Those first years, in the organizing of this educational prison ministry, were full of things to do. Things we felt would make a difference in the lives of someone behind bars. We didn't know how right we were.

We were knowledgeable enough to know education was the narrow window that would give us our best chance to make a difference, in the area of fighting cultural and historical illiteracy, functional illiteracy, and racism, afflicting our people behind bars.

First, we felt it was necessary to convince our inmate brothers and sisters it was possible for them to express themselves in print, and not in violence. This plan worked very well, making it possible to publish our first book which clearly illustrated what was possible, when those on the inside are willing to work with those on the outside for positive rewards.

Our first reward was a publication entitled "Brothers In and Out." This title got its name from part of our organization's name, and because at the time we had not made contact with any female inmates.

How cruelly and inhumanely many prison officials operate their prisons! This increased my desire to learn more, and to learn how I could make a difference in the lives of any African-American inmate who truly wanted to change their mindset.

Our first publication was a successful project with one exception—there was no input from any female inmate. One of my co-workers had information on how I could contact a woman, who had reached out to her church for fellowship. She promised to bring me the address after her next trip to her church.

True to her word, I was given the prison address of a female inmate named Rose Jones, at the California Institute for Women at Corona, California. Jones is not her last name, because I didn't seek her permission to use her given name. The important thing is she assisted our organization in building a strong prison ministry inclusive of any female that wanted our services.

Within one week after receiving this new opportunity to reach a sister inmate, I had written my first-ever letter to a female inmate. The response to this letter was somewhat like the first correspondence I sent into the Corcoran State Prison, it was received with much love.

The necessary forms were sent by Sister Rose, to get Brother Ali and myself cleared to make our first visit to the California Institute for Women, at Corona California. Three weeks later I made my first visit to a female facility.

I shall always remember my first time stepping inside of a female prison—seeing women held behind iron bars, and razor wire enclosures. Never before in my life would I have ever believed I would ever witness African–American females held prisoner. All I could think at the time, was all of these females come from families that they must have loved, and in many cases still do. I couldn't help but wonder what the hell is our country coming to, when it has to incarcerate this number of its females, due to the system failing them somewhere in their past?

Two things happened to me on that first trip. First, I met Rose, a woman who had been sent to prison for defending her life, and the lives of her family. A woman whose faith was as strong as any person I had met, since my youth and the death of my grandmother. She said Jesus would open the doors of this prison, and set her free. You only had to look into her eyes, and hear the conviction in her voice, to know her faith was real.

The second thing that endeared itself to me on that first visit, was the introduction to Romarilyn, and learning of the inside organization of which she was sitting Chairperson. Not only did I learn of the African-American Women Prison Association (AAWPA), I also met the founding staff on that occasion.

With Romarilyn and myself, an instant bond was formed, that is still in effect to this date. The AAWPA was just getting started as an organization, just as our organization was yet in its infancy. It didn't take long for the two organizations to become supportive of what each group was out to accomplish. The AAWPA had succeeded in bringing a sense of sisterhood to the inmates at that facility, unheard of in the history of California prisons for women—largely, due to Romarilyn's vision and passion for rehabilitation, for any inmate that was willing to work hard to overcome her disadvantages.

All of those involved as staff were equally committed to the task of making the most of their lives, while being locked away from their families and the outside world. Not once in the past ten years have I heard one of these sisters complain of their innocence. I only have knowledge of those that I came in contact with on what became weekly trips, as the outside sponsor for several programs organized and operated by the staff of the AAWPA.

Sister Rose was right in the midst of any activity that involved religious programs. On several occasions I was asked to speak at the prison chapel, whenever the AAWPA was hosting an event. Sister Rose was the director of the choir, and one of its lead singers. She was always busy when it came to serving her Lord and Savior Jesus Christ. It was always good to see her each time we made the weekly visits.

The AAWPA would hold several very important events in honor of the heritage of the African-American inmate. At these events our organization was always invited. In the beginning we made serious attempts to get others cleared, in order that they might accompany us for these events. This was always, and still is, a hard sell in getting our people to show a willingness to become involved with going behind prison walls, in order to show love to our inmates.

Finally, Brother Ali's application was cleared for him to visit at California Institute for Women, where I had been doing what I hoped was good liaison work between the two groups. Now we had two big brothers to assist the development of their programs for rehabilitation. These were very exciting times for both groups, as we grew in knowledge of showing our love and respect for the art of caring.

As time passed, the two groups became even closer. I looked forward to my visit each week. Being an activist in Los Angeles can be very stressful at times, especially when things are not going well in your personal relationships at home. Just being around positive African-Americans provides a release valve for me. I'm certain Brother Ali was in a somewhat similar situation.

In my early development, I received much love. My home didn't have the presence of a male adult around. Therefore, I never felt one was necessary. My mother was away working to provide for the family, her family. Living with our grandmother, there was never a

FROM MISEDUCATION TO INCARCERATION

lack of love and affection. Always in the presence of the black female, I sense an aura of nurturing; they exemplify caring. I had never given much thought to this phenomenon until I started going inside this female facility. Whenever I was in the presence of my grandmother, I could sense this phenomenon. Maybe there is something in the mirrors of my soul that reflects back to the caring and nurturing that I felt from my grandmother and other women I encountered. How much of our culture is lost for lack of knowing or wanting to know?

This caring is present among the African-American inmates at this facility. Rose is no longer there, having been released more than three years ago, still full of the faith that opened the doors and set her free. A new life has opened up to her, and she is determined to make the best of this opportunity. With this same faith intact that took her from behind prison bars, her future is very much among the blue chips in this game of life.

There are other names that have won their way into the inner recesses of my mind, only to come forward each time I hear, or read, any news about ill-treatment of female inmates. These names have faces, that are dear to me in the sense of daughters, sisters, and friends. Betty comes to my mind each time I come in contact with a female that is full of the spirit of life. She would always rush to give me a sisterly hug, before the system inserted itself in this African-American cultural tradition of showing sisterly and brotherly love, to say stop. Sister Betty, is always happy to make Brother Ali and myself know how much she and others really feel towards the two of us, for coming to visit them.

All of the miles up and down the freeways of Southern California, in bumper-to-bumper traffic, to spend less than two hours visiting in an atmosphere of Afrocentric enjoyment filled with spirituality. Some of the females of other ethnic backgrounds came to love and respect both Brother Ali and myself for our compassion.

Nothing is the same since the terrorist attack on America. Trust and love have taken a back seat to racism in America, which is now on the rise. Progress, that was once an easy call at the CIW Corona facility, towards rehabilitation came to a stop for our outside sponsorship. Now we only visit on days when the sisters in the AAWPA are having their annual events celebrating Kwanzaa, Juneteenth, Dr. Martin Luther King, Jr's, birthday, and Black History month. All other programs that our organization once provided, outside sponsorship for is ended at the moment. This is the most painful part of this fear mania that is presently choking the life out of the people, as the gods of war command center stage.

Another loss I feel is not hearing the voices in the mass choir at this female prison—one voice in particular, that of a young sister that was born into a family of gospel singers. I first became aware of her when I carried a picture of her on a poster, that briefly told her story in relationship to the three strikes law, as I marched in a protest demonstration. On my next visit following that protest, I was blessed to meet her in person, and not long after meeting her I was doubly blessed to hear her sing. Mary, is one of those specially gifted African-Americans who have the gift of song. When that gift of song is imbued with a spirit that enjoys making others happy, it's a beautiful sight, and Mary is such an individual spirit. On several occasions we talked briefly about her case, and about the mass choir—she is one of its directors. On one of these occasions she expressed to me the need for choir robes, and would my organization assist them in getting robes. Not only did I feel we would help them in this need, Brother Ali, who is now the director, felt it an honor to do so.

This need was made known to the church where I am a member. It was made known to other church groups where I often spoke at the

FROM MISEDUCATION TO INCARCERATION

time of this need. Then I went to a brother that has a business involving the craft of tailoring, to provide information on the cost of buying enough material to make robes for ninety choir members. Before this information could be provided, I left on my annual trip to visit my daughters on the east coast. On one of my frequent calls to check on the progress of the required information to get the robes for our sisters, I was given a cost figure. The brother that provided the information, would, if there was no other way, make the robes himself at cost.

Since no one else had come forward to assist in this matter, our director felt there had to be another way. Inside the facility where the sisters are incarcerated is a sweatshop where all manner of items are made for the California Department of Corrections. Several members of the AAWPA work in that shop, and provided the information that they could make the robes, if our organization could get permission for them to do so. Our director got off a letter to the Department of Corrections, requesting their permission for their sweatshop to make these robes, if NABSIO would provide the material. To our surprise, not only did they grant permission for the robes to be made in their facility, they also informed our organization that they were aware of the work we were doing inside the prison as outside sponsors. Needless to say, this was a giant step forward in our ministry's role as sponsors to the programs of the AAWPA.

My next move was to take the money out of my checking account and send it to Brother Ali. Then it was in his capable hands to get the job done. He was so successful, the sisters are still talking about their joy in being able to have a hand in making this dream a reality for all concerned.

On my return from my trip, the sisters put the mass choir out front in their own version of gospel fest. I was invited, along with Brother

Ali and another guest. All of my help in getting robes for these sisters, was rewarded many times over in seeing the pride they felt in singing with their robes on.

When Mary stepped forward to take the mike in her hands, the tears would not stay inside my eyes. I sent out a prayer for Mary to gain her freedom from the enslavement of California's three strikes law. The program was very successful, even to the newly appointed warden who was present for this occasion. There were those present that stated later, they had never heard the sisters singing as well as they did that night. I personally felt they were telling Brother Ali and me, just how thankful they were in the songs they were singing. There was no doubt in my mind, that Mary pulled out all the stops in her voice, as she looked directly at me while she was singing, which sent a warm feeling into my very being.

Chapter **13**

MEETING THE CHALLENGE

For many years the prisons across this nation, from California to New York, have held unrecorded numbers of functionally illiterate New African inmates, with little or no hope for their plight—with no one to hear their cry, or even make a feeble attempt to be fair or offer help.

You would think any help, to cause inmates to seek new mindsets, would be welcome! Not so! Already the evil forces are coming forth, in an attempt to criminalize our plans.

One method being employed is an old white supremacist dirty

FROM MISEDUCATION TO INCARCERATION

trick, calling any positive attempt to change the mindset of the New African, from that of the criminal to that of the nation builder, gang related.

What many may fail to realize is there are those New Africans who are free thinkers, that will do all in our power to break the chains of functional and cultural illiteracy, holding many black inmates behind iron bars of racist captivity. We are willing to place our very lives on the line, to assure no brother or sister is left behind that is seeking "knowledge of self."

Functional illiteracy is an equal opportunity employer. Not only is this condition widespread among inmates, it can often be found among those charged with guarding inmates. An example can be found among those guards holding down duty at the segregated housing units (SHU), at maximum-security prisons throughout America. For talking to another prisoner, an inmate can be accused of being a "gang member." For writing to an inmate that is being held under the cloud of being a gang member, you too can be under scrutiny as a gang collaborator—all because of some culturally illiterate racist guard.

Are we, the tax-paying public, to stand on the sidelines, while the game of criminal behavior goes on all around us? I think not! Meeting the challenge is a part of fighting functional illiteracy among gang members, or any other New Africans born under the cloud of continuation slavery. One of the major reasons our youth get involved with gang activity is their being miseducated in our public schools. In meeting the challenge of getting our gang members to understand how much they are hurting their people with negative behavior, we are handicapped by not being able to reach out to them through the written word.

The problem with those who are afflicted with white supremacy in America, and other areas where the European man is in power, is

MEETING THE CHALLENGE

they believe the ability to think rests only with them.

Getting our people who are living the life of criminals, to see another way, will not be an easy task. There are many New Africans who are as destructive to the black community, as any white supremacist could ever be. They live among their people and are in the position to cause harm—selling drugs, raping our women, killing innocent people with no remorse. Meeting this challenge is not something the New African can any longer leave in the hands of those that don't have our best interests as a high priority.

Fighting our way out of this miseducation abyss will take a major effort by all New Africans. Just the ones with the guts to step up to the plate, in this game of life, from the pits of hell locked down in prison, will not be enough for this army. Yet, these are the ones that can set the pace that we can follow, if we will but hear their voices crying out from behind prison walls. They want to come back into the bosom of Mother Blackness as builders, and not the destroyers that miseducation shaped them to become.

It is a waste of valuable time fighting needless battles with white supremacy, when the real fight is to win the minds of our people to the point of clarity, where all New Africans can see the lack of knowledge is killing our people. White supremacy, in and of itself, is not and never will be the killer that lack of knowledge is, among New African people here in this land that is devoid of love for its descendants, whose foreparents provided the free labor that got this nation off and running. Prison slavery, is the number one use this nation has for the New African.

This battle is being waged among, and for, the have-nots in this nation—for people where drugs is a way of life, where death can take out a family member without prior notice. Where children attend school in classrooms that are only a shade better equipped than many classrooms in Third World schools. They are inadequate for educat-

FROM MISEDUCATION TO INCARCERATION

ing children operating at the genius level, but, more than adequate to continue to miseducate students that are functional illiterates, just the right level for serving a life sentence behind bars in America's new slave system.

Meeting this challenge is a part of the long and continuous struggle to return our people to a position of greatness. It's a vital part of a people's right to fight with all their strength against any foe, no matter the price that must be paid, to right the wrongs of taking a people against their will. As many of the "haves" in this nation celebrate this holiday season, many of the "have-nots" find it hard to put food on their table. One cannot help but wonder at times, just what value are the holiday seasons to those living below the poverty line that separates the "haves" from the "have-nots."

From day one, after the Portuguese barbarians came to the continent of Africa, this struggle has been a continuous uphill battle by a people that have withstood some of the worst treatment known to mankind, at the hands of people with ice water flowing through their veins.

The trailblazers for this struggle to meet the challenge, confronting the twin killers in functional and cultural illiteracy, extend from ancient Egypt to the present. Even European scholars had to recognize the genius of Imhotep. Just as they had to recognize the scholarship of Dr. W.E.B. DuBois, and the African scholar, Cheikh Anta Diop—New Africans that took a backseat to no man, black or white. They were always on the cutting edge of any literary struggle that was righteous for the upliftment of people of color. These are the footprints we must walk in to bring the George Jackson University, into the forefront in our fight against the evils found in functional and cultural illiteracy.

In meeting this challenge, we must accept the teachings of our most notable scholar, Dr. Maulana Karenga, who gave us the second principle of the Nguzo Saba, which is Kujichagulia (self-determination). When truly understood, it says we have the right, "To define ourselves, create for ourselves and speak for ourselves." From this enlightened state of movement there is offered a new definition for the Africans born in America, from the brothers in the Missouri State Penitentiary that says:

New African is a non-sectarian term that recognizes the unique evolution of our people here in America. <u>We are New Africans because we are an African people who have evolved from the bloody Trans-Atlantic slave trade and centuries of chattel slavery here in North America, that effected several African nations.</u> It is an irrefutable historical fact that our African ancestors, who were kidnapped and enslaved here in America, came from various tribes such as: the Yoruban, Ibos, Ashantis and many more.

All of these African people, by forced and unforced circumstances, through intermarriages, sexual relations and the mass rape of African women by their European slave masters, were fused into a new people, <u>thus forming a New African nation here in North America.</u>

So when we use the term New African we are identifying and taking into consideration all of the Africans who were brought to America, forced into chattel slavery, and biologically mixed, as opposed to a particular sect or tribe. Under our ideological concept, you can be a New African Christian, a New African Muslim or simply a New African. Your religion is your own personal relationship with the Creator. It does not matter to us what your religious persuasion is. What is essential to the revolution and complete liberation of our people is that we embrace a distinct identity from that given to us by our oppressor—an identity that we can assert before the world and be proud of.

THAT NATIONAL IDENTITY IF "NEW AFRICAN" I AM A NEW AFRICAN!!

    This definition is inserted in this book, to let the reader know just how serious meeting the challenge of standing together truly is for the New African thinking inmate. And we do see ourselves as New Africans. We will write to whoever needs us, no matter what the oppressor may call this New African inmate. We cannot let the fear of negative stigmatization cause us to alter our course, or change our mission. The road ahead will not be an easy one. Nor has the history of the New African been an easy road up from the initial contact with the European oppressors.

    It is important that we get inside the minds of those wanting to embrace this definition, in order to advance in unity. To give this definition the respect it rightfully deserves, we must usher in a new day among New African inmates locked down, throughout America's new slave plantation, its prison system.

    I close as I came, embracing all New African thinkers, that rush to close ranks around our functionally and culturally illiterate brothers and sisters, who desperately need our help. **AND THEY SHALL HAVE IT!!!**

BOOK AVAILABLE THROUGH
Milligan Books, Inc.
An Imprint of Professional Business Consulting Service
From Miseducation to Incarceration $13.95

Order Form

Milligan Books, Inc.
1425 W. Manchester Ave., Suite C, Los Angeles, CA 90047
(323) 750-3592

Name_____ Date _____

Address_____

City_____ State____ Zip Code _____

Day Telephone _____

Evening Telephone _____

Book Title_____

Number of books ordered___ Total ....$ _____

Sales Taxes (CA Add 8.25%) ....$ _____

Shipping & Handling $4.90 for one book ..$ _____

Add $1.00 for each additional book ....$ _____

Total Amount Due.......................................$ _____

☐ Check ☐ Money Order ☐ Other Cards _____

☐ Visa   ☐ MasterCard Expiration Date _____

Credit Card No. _____

Driver License No. _____

Make check payable to Milligan Books, Inc.

_____   _____

Signature   Date